Was that a Compliment?

Was that a Compliment?

And Other Themes of My 20s

By Whitney Wilson

Illustrations by:
Liz Taylor

Photographs by:
Christie Mumm, JLM Creative Photography

To the ADVO Crew:

I could not have spent my 20s in a better way,
with better people.

Advocating for the name and ways of Jesus with you was
the "immeasurably more" Paul talks about in Ephesians 3:20.

Faith and freedom. Dancing dodgeball.
Coffee and camaraderie. Straight grace.

I wish you could see how big I smile when I talk about you!

Table of Contents

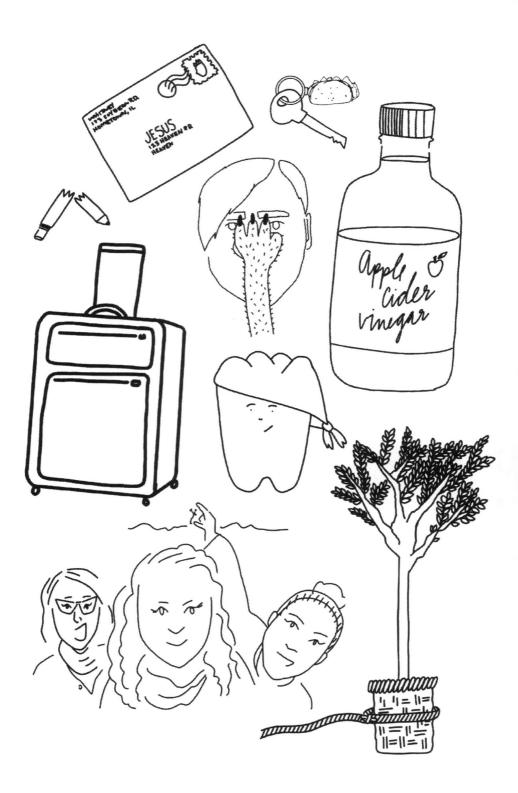

Introduction

No one asked me to write a book. I do not know if I am supposed to write a book. I do not know the first thing about writing or editing or publishing or selling a book. I read other people's books, and I write journal entries, and I don't even edit my text messages well (or should I say we'll).

I have always wanted to write a book, but wanting to write a book and knowing what to write about are not the same thing.

Because I work in ministry, I have had ideas for books before. Well, I have had ideas for *titles* of books before.

To name a few:

- *How to Start a Ministry with 30 People and Just Sort of Keep It There*

- *I Really Thought More People Would Be Into This: The Ministry Events of Whitney Wilson*

- *100 Things Not to Say to Single People* (and its sequel: *Yes, I Have Heard of Christian Mingle*)

- *Do Not Have a Yard Sale – and Other Lessons Learned in Student Ministry*

- *Hoard for the Lord: A Pictorial of Church Basements* (Foreword by Oriental Trading)

Look for those at a future date.

This book did not start with a title. It started with a realization. A realization I was turning 30.

The "dirty 30" thing had not bothered me. I am a big believer in my best years being ahead.

When I really think about it, I wouldn't want to be younger anyway. My early 20s contained plenty of me at my "not best," and most of the time, I have zero desire to go back there.

But one day, in the middle of my 29'ness, it hit hard that this whole 20s thing was wrapping up.

Soon, I would walk the stage of an invisible graduation, where each birthday card would be like a creased diploma signifying the end of a decade and the turning over of a significant season. Time would reach up and transfer the tassel on my 20s hat as a handful of years, one for each finger currently typing, would expire.

There had been so much packed in these years. What did I get to take with me? Anything?

According to a horrifying article I read titled "What Happens to Your Body After 30," there are plenty of physiological things I would not carry into my 30s.[1] But I did not have to read it to know I'm aging. All the signs are there.

The ability to eat fast food at midnight has long gone. Sleeping past 8 a.m. is no longer a treat but a reason to panic. "Nothing" has become a favorite thing to do. I do not know popular music. I pick up on slang about 18 months too late. The Tupperware aisle at TJ Maxx is my favorite aisle at TJ Maxx.

Youth is going the way of RadioShack, and its products are falling off my truck and into the rearview mirror with every mile. To be fair, there are plenty of things I am happy to leave behind with my 20s.

Insecurities. Failures. Fears. Faults. Jealousies. Comparisons. Pseudo-maturity. Way-too-thin eyebrows.

But there is a souvenir suitcase I am packing to take with me, full of themes. Themes like treasures, buried in these precious years, hidden to be found along the path, dug up by both excruciating work and great joy. They have not been perfected but have been polished repeatedly by light, grace, and truth – washed in the ordinary days of experience, discovered along daily attempts at following Jesus.

Some are hard to look at, still. Some make me smile.
Some bring painful memories. Others carry real joy.

But they all bring freedom. They all reveal truth. They all find their casting in God's wisdom and their breath in Scripture's living insight.

In this book, I have gone through my 20s closet, discarded all I no longer need, and gathered up what remains and what is unequivocally valuable to my soul, my character, my hope, my relationships, and my faith.

I am hoping all this sorting and naming and storing of the themes of my 20s will not just be for my benefit. I am hoping it will be for yours, too. I am hoping it reads deeper than advice and touches on something more pure and lasting.

Advice can be good, of course, but it can also be situational.

There are plenty of insights we can share with one another that are specific to our life stage, class distinction, and cultural context. Advice can apply now but not then. It may be good for me but will not work for you. It may speak well to a certain part of the world and fall dead at the door to those living on the other side of it.

Truth, on the other hand, is always true.

It does not pick and choose or play favorites. It cannot be shaped, tailored, or bribed. It is constant. It is foundational. It is eternal. It is gravity, and it is grace. No matter where you were born or who you were born to. No matter how much money you have or what you scored on your A.C.T.

In this book, I have attempted to gather up the themes I have repeatedly turned to, given out, and found to be true. To put their weight on paper and bind them with grace and gratitude.

This is my capsule wardrobe of repeated truths. The staple pieces. The garments that didn't wear out after plenty of use.

If we were gathered over cookies and coffee talking about life, each of these themes is something I would confidently look you in the eye and say, "There are a lot of things I do not have figured out yet, but I can tell you: this is **TRUE**."

So, take it from someone who knows how to start a ministry with 30 people and just sort of keep it there: advice is nice, but truth makes all the difference. It is no wonder the Bible talks so much about it.

Chapter One
Extra Sandwiches and a Merry McRibmas

It is weird to write a memoir-ish type book when I have not really accomplished anything of memoir-ness.

Diagnosed with a debilitating illness? Nope. Moved to a developing nation and alleviated generational poverty and oppression? Notta. Have a wunderkind level knowledge of finance, science, nutrition, or anything remotely impressive that actually sells books? Nothin'.

Sure, I have several not-quite-qualifications for writing a book.

I once started a YouTube channel and raced my way to 27 subscribers (and I think I am one of them). I took home a "Participant" trophy in Wayne County's Little Miss Bean Queen contest circa 1993.[2] I formerly had visions of a snow cone empire before barely breaking even on the school carnival and rummage sale circuit and packing up the syrup and funnel cups for good – in a dumpster, because I could not handle the pressure.

Technically, I am a published writer.

I appeared in *Scholastic News* in the 4th grade for a piece I wrote on blue-tailed skinks. Maybe you heard about it. It included the line, "Get a load of this!" Demonstrating another not-quite-qualification: I say dumb stuff.

Once a guy at my church called me, "Chicago Girl" because the fact I had lived in Chicagoland was the only thing he could remember about me. I, in a panic to think of a comeback nickname, remembered his first name started with a P, and responded, "Hey, P...man."

"P Man?? Did I just say...P Man?"

Or the time in 3rd grade my brother picked me up from school and offered to also give a ride to a cute, popular boy in the grade ahead of me. Luckily I was at that age when I had no idea how to interact with cute boys.[3]

My dad was a high school basketball coach, which meant I would be at the school late while his team practiced. My mom would pack me an extra sandwich and a Capri Sun in a paper bag to take along for the supping. I fatefully had the lunch sack with me this day, loading into my brother's car.

"What's up?" the cool boy said, as he leaned the front seat forward, so I could crawl into the back.

I mistakenly heard him say, "What's that?" and thought he was referencing my lunch sack.

"An extra sandwich," I sheepishly responded.

My brother shot a look in the rearview mirror like I was lame in human form and said, "Whit. He said, 'WHAT IS UP.'"

If I could have crawled under the seat or jumped from the moving vehicle or been transported to a planet incapable of sustaining human life, I would have.

"What's up?" – cool boy
"An extra sandwich." – me

Cringe.

The most literal dumb thing I ever said was at Steak 'n Shake with my college friends.

It was our favorite hang out. The wait staff would occasionally sneak us a midnight bowl of chili while charging us for a *cup* of chili, winking with an air of, "Let's keep this between us."

Our low-grade meat cup runneth over.

Side note: This was also the scene of our one attempt at the "gallon challenge." Trying to drink a gallon of milk in under an hour (whole at that – because we aren't posers) is horrifying enough, but to add to the entertainment, we snuck a goldfish into the jug of our friend Brady.

He chugged. It surfaced. He insta-milk-puked all over the Steak 'n Shake parking lot.

Our Steak 'n Shake soirees would start around 11 p.m. We would stay until 2 or 3 a.m. – laughing, telling stories, daring each other to eat those green peppers they keep on the table. We did this way more nights than not.

The early a.m. is not my peak operating time. You know people who don't hold their liquor well? Well, I don't hold my tired well. My brain turns to slosh. I get cranky, unreasonable, and easily confused.

One of these nights, over soupy milkshakes and room-temp chili mac, we discussed that mind-blowing television phenomena when characters from a TV show make a guest appearance *in character*, on another show.

Ref: when *Family Matters* character Steve Urkel appeared on *Full House,* blowing my 6 year old mind to BITS.[4] I could not believe what I saw. Did the Tanners even comprehend the miracle and inception before them? This had to be described somewhere in Revelation. No matter what, Jesus was involved and must have loved T.G.I.F.

In my defense, this *is* what we were talking about. But somewhere, the subject matter changed, and I missed it.

What I did not miss was one of my friends saying, "I couldn't believe it when I realized the dad from Stuart Little is Dr. House from *House!*"

Of course, what my friend referred to is how Hugh Laurie, the actor who plays Dr. House on the show "House," also plays Mr. Little in the 90's movie version of the E.B. White classic. But I was tired. And slow. And oh, so confused.

8

I sat back in my sticky Steak 'n Shake seat, trying to comprehend what was being said. In a moment of intensity (and soon-to-be regret), I believed I was being hoodwinked and spoke up.

"Wait. What?" – me, snarkily, with an "I'm on to you" tone.

"Yeah! 'House' is Stuart Little's dad." – my friend, reassuringly.

"So. Wow. Ok. You expect me to believe that Dr. House – the brilliant, miracle working, talented-but-troubled doctor extraordinaire – is actually the father of a tiny, little, talking MOUSE?!"

*Cue everyone at the table squinting, in pained disbelief, trying to determine if I had a stroke or am the dumbest friend they have ever had or if the gallon challenge had cognitive effects, and I should be submitted for medical research.

I quickly came to my senses, and simultaneously caught on to what they had meant and to what I had actually said. A haunting voice in my head hissed, *"Extra sandwich. Extra sandwich. Extra sandwichhhhhh."*

Humility, you are a doll and a half. I would punch Stuart Little in the face if I had the chance.

In addition to the already shared "not-quite-qualifications" for writing a book, I am also a walking *Was that a compliment?*

*Was that a compliment?*s happen when someone offers an observational statement to you about you, and you can tell they mean it as a positive, but it still kind of feels like a tiny punch in the insecurity pouch.

It is a well-meaning insult.

Like the time a lady walked up to me after I sang and commented on my "husky" voice. For the good of (wo)mankind everywhere, let's keep husky reserved solely to a dog breed and nothing that would ever be used to describe anything about a woman. Ever. And all the altos said, "Amen."

Or the night a friend remarked on my outfit and followed it up with, "You always look so COMFY!" The internal translation will always be FRUMPY. That I always look frumpy.

Or the time another friend visited a popular American city. I asked about her trip and what she thought of the city.

"Actually, it reminded me a lot of you!
You know, how you are both quirky."

Quirky? Really? Because, actually, no. I did not know! Could have went with "fun" or "fresh" or "inviting" – but nope. Quirky. A word mostly associated with "weird."

Or when I went to pick out my first pair of new glasses in years, back home in southern Illinois.

I headed to the cheapo section and tried on some black (what I thought to be fashionable and safe) thick rims and took them to the glasses technician.

Here I was, thinking I was joining the modern glasses movement – channeling Tina Fey and the other cute glasses pioneers who have gone before me! Instead, the tech started to process the order, took a look at my choice, and said, "Oh. Do you want to see some of our more feminine options?"

Silly me with my macho man glasses! I wanted to whip out Taylor Swift's Instagram right then and there. Did she not know how "in" these were? Did she not know thick frames are not

just for Austin Powers anymore? I went from feeling like
T. Swizzle to Woody Allen in a moment. Sheesh on sheesh.

Maybe southern Illinois is not a hotbed for cutting edge
eyewear. Apparently it is for *Was that a compliment?*s.

Like McDonald's on Christmas Eve.[5]

I wish I was the kind of person who thinks McDonald's is gross.
While I am at it, I wish I was the kind of person who genuinely
prefers dark chocolate to milk; who says, "There's no way I'll
finish this!" when a restaurant meal comes; or who finds the
gym "therapeutic" and Whole 30 "worth it."

Alas, I am not that person.

So, when my friends and I needed a meal source on
Christmas Eve and McDonald's was the only alternative
to cooking one ourselves, I was all for it.

I ordered and stood waiting for my food. The employee called
out, "McRib! Order up!" I did not respond.

My friend Craig said, "Whitney, isn't that yours?"

What? Craig thinks I ordered a McRib?

"No?" I said confused.

"Oh. I just thought that is what you would order."

Craig looked down and away, with all the guise of someone
who had betrayed a friend.

"Wait. Craig. WAIT! Are you saying I just seem like the type of girl who would order a McRib?? Like, that is just a safe assumption?"

Craig shrugged his shoulders and gave a face like that is not what he was not saying, and we somehow maintained a friendship – because Jesus is alive and deep calls out to processed meat deep.

For the record, regardless of my Midwest roots or the fact that I know a decent amount about professional wrestling,[6] I do not eat McRibs.

Husky. Comfy. Quirky. McRibby.

I am surprised I'm not more insecure than I am.

And really, isn't that a *Was that a compliment?* in itself?

It could also be the only qualification I have to write this book: I am not nearly as insecure as I should be.

My 20s brought plenty of reasons to be insecure. Jesus kept giving better and more beautiful themes to pursue.

And I am grateful. Because I, like parties, need a theme.

Chapter Two
Every Party Needs a Theme

I do not like answering the "introvert vs. extrovert" question, because I do not think we have to be one or the other. I think we can be part-time. Or at least 80/20. I am that: a switch hitter in where I get refueled and recharged.

There are plenty of times I draw strength and become "the most me" when contemplative, in quiet, in the woods, in a bookstore's back booth, in solitude. I can get down with a Moleskin and black coffee afternoon with the best of them.

But there are other times that hit like lightning. When it is people – not silence, not coffee, not instrumental soundtracks or intellectual retreats – that bring the energy that lights up my mind's sky and make it exciting to be alive.

When the room is made bright and loud and beautiful and electric by the people and stories and banter and laughter it holds. When fun is in full color and full of personalities.

Sometimes in just the right room with just the right people, it seems like I back up against a light switch in my soul, and something is flipped and friends are my most favorite thing and we cannot laugh hard enough and we cannot make someone feel welcome enough and we cannot have too many pizza rolls or party games. When 2 liters stack like bowling pins on a counter and a dance party can break out at any moment.

Oh. I. Love. That.

Filling a place with friends and friends-to-be and setting off friendship fireworks.

I have hosted many of these gatherings, and when I do, there is one thing I need – that I depend on. More than 2 liters. More than streamers. More than a guest list or Facebook event. Yes, even more than Pinterest. (Gasp!)

It is a theme. I need a theme.
Every party needs a theme.

A theme is my North Star. A theme dictates the main story line and gives me what all the other components support and point toward. A theme tells me what decorations to buy, what the invitations should look like, what everyone should wear, what food to cook,[7] what music to play, and what games to make everyone suffer through.

I get excited about a theme. I find peace in a theme. That peace and excitement push me towards completion.

Why just casually invite friends over to watch an award show in humdrum get ups, like we do not need a name for the night that rhymes, when we could be getting together for a Grammy Pajammie Party?? Where (you guessed it) we watch the Grammys, in our pajammies. A gathering in adult onesies while dancing to live music performances, as I prophesy about the return of Justin Bieber and how everyone will regret not jumping on the bandwagon when I did. That is a night no longer unpurposed. #BeliebMe

Who wants to have a blasé barbecue when one run to Dollar Tree could turn that shindig into a Quinceañera Mardi Gras Luau? (Because my friends and I cannot decide which decorations to buy in the party aisle, so we buy them all. The theme could also be: "Indecision.") Prepare yourself for the best Spanish fan/string bead/grass skirt combination a dollar can turn out. It is a backyard cultural casserole. Yum.

If you get invited to my house for a Comfy Clothes Hangout (capital letters + at least one alliteration = theme town = party ready), you best show up in anti-pants and something to dip in Nutella, because this is no longer an aimless hang out. You are part of a party, friend.

If it is October and I live in Florida and I need to pretend like there is a season other than "Hot and humid" vs "A little less hot, still humid," you are coming over for a Fake Fall Bash!

We will commission a hayride out of a friend's Jeep and tiny trailer that is far from street legal but no one needs to know, and we will sweat it out in our flannel, jeans, and cute scarves in the 90s for the sake of the pictures.

I will clean up hay and candy corn and Mason jars moldy with old apple cider in my house for months – and love it.

Because I love themes, and I love parties.
And every party needs a theme.

...

Middle school girls and a summer camp version of water polo taught me the power and importance of a theme.

The first time I got asked to be a middle school summer camp sponsor, I only said yes because I did not know if I was allowed to say no. I was new to a church staff and had not yet learned the rules of what was expected and what my position would entail or not entail. Not wanting to come across as a non-team player and hoping to appear as more of a servant than I am, I signed on for summer camp, somewhat reluctantly, having never really worked with the wild and wonderful world of middle schoolers before. My only experience was when I was one and that was not great.

Per ush, the Lord knows what we need and what we will love better than we do. It became one of the best weeks of my life.

I came back with 70 new best friends, an increased tolerance for heat and B.O. (it was Florida, in July, with those in puberty), probably some poison ivy, and definitely more stories than a heart can hold.

I do not know what kind of summer camps you grew up going to, but for this one, camp competition is BIG LEAGUE.

We divide into teams. We acquire points. We keep track of scores. We are out to obliterate opponents.

If it were possible to watch game film of human Foosball and four-way Ultimate Frisbee to fine tune our technique and develop tighter strategy, we would. If there were scouting reports available for carpet ball, we would pour over them. There is no limit to the number of four square fights and controversies I have refereed/been a part of.[8]

The winning team gets much more than their name announced at closing camp ceremonies. There is an entire year's worth of bragging rights on the table. The victory team members strutting into youth group the next week wearing their team-colored bandanas and waving their team flag is a beautiful, hallowed thing. Who does not want those rights? Who does not want that strut?

When we first unloaded the bus at Lakewood Retreat, we got our team assignments as counselors and huddled with our kids. My particular team did not look promising.

Our competitive edge was, in a word, yikes.

In what I believe to be a grand conspiracy from the camp organizer, we were made up of nearly all fresh-faced 6th grade girls who looked like they wanted to go ahead and phone in a stomachache for every sporting activity.

It was the kind of team that made me think, *"Maybe we will do really well at trivia!"* and desperately ask the point keeper, "You are going to award points for random acts of kindness,* right?"

*As I strategically calculate random acts of kindness to be done in front of the point keepers. ("Oh, my girl picked up a chip bag from the ground and walked it to the trash! That was pretty RANDOMLY KIND, wouldn't ya say??" *wink)

We did have one super athlete on our team – a male counselor, who conveniently, the week before camp, got a bum ankle and would not be participating in any rec activities.

I prepared myself for a week of beatdowns and no opportunities to trash talk.

Pacing beside the pool for our first bout of water polo, I had no idea what to do. I was Gordon Bombay in *Mighty Ducks*,[9] needing to teach these kids a water polo equivalent of a flying V. How would we prove we were not a bunch of cake eaters? The ice was thin and the water, treacherous.

Camp water polo is terrifying. Limbs bend like pipe cleaners, as you swallow copious amounts of pool water hundreds of students use as their only bathing agent for the week. This is *300* starring a cast of manic, unhinged pre-teens who are playing for SPARTA. There are zero rules.

"Try not to drown someone."

That is about it. The goal is to get the big, red kickball through the cones set up as goals any way you can.

You can imagine how horrified my team of newbies were watching this bloodbath and then having to play. Have you ever seen tree frogs cling to a windowsill? Now picture those frogs utterly panicked, where the ground is lava, and to slip from the windowpane is to land in the fiery abyss.

There you have a decent picture of our team. Wall clinging. Eyes shut. Guttural whimpers.[10]

For these girls, the poolside was their windowsill and to let go was to be carried off into Polo Persia.

Meanwhile, it looked like a one-way all star game for the other team. We got scored on mercilessly, as our opponents practiced their trick shots, victory dances, and getting everyone on their team involved. (*"Oh good. The kid who has never scored a point in any sporting event ever just hat-tricked on us."*)

If there were an equivalent of warm-up suits for water polo, the other teams would have never taken theirs off.

I did not blame the girls for being scared, for gluing their bodies to the safety of the pool's edge and digging their fingers into the concrete. I also knew that while this felt like the camp experience necessary for survival in the moment, it was not the camp experience they would ultimately want and delight in.

I did not know how to help them get off the wall and into the game. Unless I could give them a theme.

The scoring, the defending, the chlorinated anarchy, the other kids who looked like they knew what they were doing, the sideline experienced 7th and 8th graders barking strategy and critiques and battle cries like stage parents. The water polo package was too much. They were so daunted by everything that it kept them from doing anything. Could we simplify?

At half time, we rounded up.

"Girls. I know this is miserable. I am really proud of you for sticking it out. We cannot forfeit." (I had already checked.)

"This next half, we may not be able to score, but we can at least try to keep them from scoring. Here's what I want you to do: see the big, red kickball?" (The answer up to that point would have been "No," since they had not even turned around to face the game while we had been playing.)

19

"Anywhere that ball is, is where I want you to be. If someone is holding the ball, swarm them. If they pass the ball, swarm who they pass it to. Be where the ball is. All over it. At all times. Wherever I see the ball, I expect to see all of you on top of it. Bat at it. Bite at it. Belly flop on it. If someone is holding it, stand on their head if you have to. Do not worry about the score. Do not worry about the other kids yelling at you what to do. Just be where the ball is, and keep it from going near the goal!"

And. It. Worked. (Quack, quack, quack....)

Not in the way that we won or scored or were even competitive. But in the way that *they got in the game*. They played, had fun, experienced camp, and had stories to tell and bruises to show. They did not sideline the battle or fake a stomachache. They went where the ball was, and it got them off the wall and into the action.

I am not a water polo tactician – to clear up any rumors.
I simply know the power of a theme.

Walking with the Lord through my 20s has been like getting huddled over at various half times – when it is evident I am drowning in the intimidation and scope of the game, and I need a theme.

When I am doing horribly on my own to try and figure out the goal or the strategy or how to win. When I wall cling for fear of getting battered by the other players. When I tree frog because I do not want to make a dumb move. When I grip the concrete because the risk of losing is greater than the thrill of playing. When I contemplate getting out and drying off, because I am confused about what team I play for and why it matters.

It is then Jesus reminds me I do not need to worry about scoring or scouting or winning or strutting or concerning myself with what other players do. He does not lay out a master plan of intricately woven calculations or speak in a language I can't understand or draw up confusing plays I must execute perfectly or be benched.

His way, His wisdom, His path to life shows me big, red kickballs and says, "Go for *this!*"

"This" is not, "Go for impressive!" or "Go for being the best!"

"This" is love. In Jesus, every play called is for love. Love for God and love for people.

"This" is faithfulness. Showing up. Not quitting on mercy and compassion. Enduring when outcomes do not match expectations.

"This" is godliness. Aiming for God's-likeness in character and conduct. Doing the humble work of holiness, no matter what pool I am in.

On mission, I am back in the game. I am ready. I see the big, red kickballs. I know what to do, even if I do not know what it will do. That is no longer my mission.

My mission is: be loving, be faithful, be godly.

I am focused. I am excited. I am off the wall and into the water. These missions make me new. A tree frog turned Spartan!

A Spartan who gets bruised, takes hits, swallows water, and makes mistakes that can leave sideline commentators wincing.

But I am PLAYING, and I will have stories to tell because of it, and I will look to my coach when I get overwhelmed and need to be reminded of what the theme is in the chaos.

I love how Jesus themes out my life – how whether or not I will be found "winning" is not determined by a scoreboard (that does not exist) but by my faithfulness to the mission given in the huddles with His word and His Spirit.

These are not fancy things. These are not flashy missions. Sometimes they get sleepy in my soul.

They turn pastel and yawn.

Sometimes a mission like "love" sounds good but vague…
Like if I called a huddle with the 6th grade tree frogs and said, "Here is the game plan: WIN THE GAME!!"

It is a good thing to fist-pump to, but it will not put a play in motion to achieve it.

When the kickballs of love, faithfulness, and godliness feel like they are floating overhead, like balloons I am not sure how to reach, the letter of Colossians comes and pulls them down and puts them at eye level.

"Therefore, as God's chosen people, holy and dearly loved, clothe yourselves with compassion, kindness, humility, gentleness, and patience." Colossians 3:12, NIV

Clothe yourselves with…
Theme yourselves with…

Compassion. Kindness. Humility. Gentleness. Patience.

These are the attributes of love, the clothing of faithfulness, and the uniform for godliness. And I know what they look like. I know what they require of me. I know how to bat them, swarm them, and stand on their heads.

When I am not sure how to handle a situation, when I feel like I cannot win and the other side is too daunting, when I cannot remember who I am and who I am supposed to be, when the water is brutal and the competition is fierce ...

When I am caught in doubt or despair, when I am so aware of my own sin and how far I am from the sanctification I crave and see clearly my own inadequacy in the game...

Every day, every interaction, every attitude, and every disappointment is an opportunity to clothe myself with these themes – in order to serve the holy assignments Jesus gives in His name to bring the Kingdom of Heaven to earth.

The power of a theme.

It is why I would not serve quesadillas and hire a Mariachi band for the Fake Fall Bash. They do not go with the theme.

In the same way, if something I want to say or do conflicts with love, with faithfulness, with godliness – if an impulse or reaction is not compassionate, kind, humble, gentle, and patient – then I need to put it back on the shelf. I have themes to serve! And I have the plays to get there.

To serve anything contrary to the theme is to lose sight of the ball and live like the huddles did not happen. I am never without a theme when I am in Christ.

I am never wandering around aimlessly at life's party store, hoping to land on something.

I am never confined to the wall, for fear I will not be good enough or strong enough to win the game. I need never cling to the concrete like I do not have a mission in the water.

Pursuing love, I have a mission. Pursuing faithfulness, I have a purpose. Pursuing godliness, I have a theme.

I have a way to dress, decorations to buy, food to serve, and invitations to send. I have pictures to take and memories to make. I have a way to treat people. I have characteristics to develop and water to play in. I have the kickballs to go after and no score to keep. And I have a summer camp and 6th grade Spartans to thank for it.

There are a lot of things to pursue in life that would be interesting for a while – maybe even impressive for a while – but would be ultimately lousy themes.

I do not know anyone who hopes the themes of their life will be stingy, selfish, insecure, untrustworthy, cowardly, or arrogant.

Who and what we serve will determine the themes of our lives.

In Christ, we get to be known for compassion, kindness, humility, gentleness, and patience – by putting His word into practice and abandoning the lesser themes of fear, pride, comparison, and selfishness.

This is the gift of grace.

This is Jesus taking our theme of sin and self preoccupation and giving us His theme of righteousness. That we may clothe ourselves in what lasts, in what matters to God and serves other people, because ultimately, these will be the only themes that matter.

24

See the big, red kickballs? Love. Faithfulness. Godliness.

Let's swarm them. Bat at them. Belly flop them. Stand on their heads if we have to and drown out every voice telling us this is not a game worth playing, and we are better off out of the pool.

Let's get off the wall and into the game. We have a theme, and we have the uniforms to put on and serve it alone.

For Sparta!

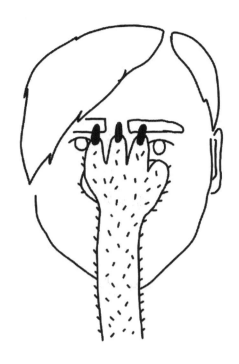

Chapter Three
Panda Paws and the Doctrine of Laughter

"One of the delightful discoveries along the way of Christian discipleship is how much enjoyment there is, how much laughter you hear, how much sheer fun you find."
– Eugene Peterson[11]

There is so much grace in laughter. It is one of my favorite realities. I feel like God designed my soul with a gauge that measures how much laughter I have put in my tank, and I can physically feel when it is getting low.

I know the friends I need to call to get it refilled, the stories I need to hear again to power back, the observational commentary that needs to take place to care for my soul.

Humor feels like coming home. It is the driveway back to my heart where I never feel lost.

Laughing. It is the best.

I do not have a distinct laugh. I am envious of my friends who do. If I could download one, I would, because I think our laughs are so important. They are the singing voices of our soul.

It is sad to me we no longer know each other's handwriting. Basically, if I have made a friend after 2005, we have had no reason to physically write anything to each other – and because of that, I might know their signature texting acronyms or spirit emojis but no longer their distinctive handwriting. So, that is how I think of a person's laugh – as their heart writing. And that is why I love the laughter of the people I love.

One of the greatest (and most fun) realizations I had in my 20s is that God cares about laughter. I knew He was fine with it before. Like coleslaw on a dinner table. It's ok if it's there, but it's ok if it's not. Laughter would never be a priority, a mark of His people, something He brings to the existential BBQ. It is just something that happened in creation – take it or leave it.

Surely the joy He spoke of is more of a subdued calm.

As though someone would be able to say, "I have joy in the Lord," without exclamation, with a period on the sentence, with a sober demeanor and somber face, and the Lord would think, "Bingo. That is what I am after."

28

Laughter was for the immature, I thought. Those who have not delved into what really matters in life. Like maybe, if you want to know how close to the Lord someone is, just notice how much they don't laugh – and that probably means they are in tune with something deeper and more godly.

What a perfect road I had laid for God to blow up and reveal a slip 'n slide underneath. He lit that fuse using student conference hilarity, Phil Wickham, and a youth group maneuver known as the Panda Paw.

I do not know if our youth group invented the Panda Paw or if we borrowed it from another. Passed down from some conference to another camp to another lock-in, eventually landing in our laps. Youth groups have a way with common denominators. It seems like a Master "Don't Call Yourself a Youth Group if You Don't Have/Do/Say These Things" pack is handed to every student leader.

It features all the games, catch phrases, and time passers to keep in our pockets and distribute to the next generation who will pass it on to the next. Different denominations, locations, and decades...same pocket fillers.

I think the pack has a paraphrase of the Deuteronomy 11 verses:

"Teach these to your students, talking about them when you sit uncomfortably on bean bags, and when you eat Chick-Fil-A, and when you think a lock-in is a good idea. You shall write them on the doorposts of splatter painted church basement walls lined with inspirational posters from the local Bible Bookstore, and use them as a diversion on the long road to Winter Jam."

The pack includes marshmallows for Chubby Bunny, a deck of cards for Mafia, examples of signs to use in "Signs," 2 liters of Mt. Lightning and Dr. Thunder, boxy tee shirts for girls to wear on water trips, a gift certificate to Little Caesars, episodes of *McGee and Me* for nostalgia night, instructions for how to get away with a "Fall Costume Party" that is NOT associated with Halloween, and phrases like "modest is hottest."

I am not sure if the Panda Paw is a part of this pack and thus, in other youth groups, but I do know when our youth group attended BigStuf 2013, a conference hosting hundreds of students in Daytona Beach, Florida – the Panda Paw came with us, revolutionizing our youth group and in fun irony, my life and opinion of God's people and laughter.

Quickly upon arrival, after checking into our hotel, divvying out room assignments, explaining to kids they will not die if not assigned to the same room as their current BFF, and buying groceries for the week,[12] the Panda Paw Challenges began.

If you did not spend the bulk of your 20s corralling 12 year olds, let me explain what a "Panda Paw" is.

A Panda Paw takes place when you walk up to a person – any person with a face will do – and moderately (not too slowly, but not too swiftly) drag your pointer, middle, and ring fingers down their confused face. Forehead to chin. A light trace down their T-zone.

Reaching the bridge of the nose, you say, "Panda Paw," and then walk away. It is like a gentler, more facially featured relative of "Cow Bite" or "Awkward Salmon." Bonus points if you are practicing on yourself right now.

It has it all in terms of youth group lore.

Disregard to personal space (check).
No explanation or reason (check).
Infectious repeatability (checkity check check).

What a Panda Paw is: stupid fun. What a Panda Paw is not: something you do to Phil Wickham. (We'll get there.)

During down time at the conference, we instituted "Panda Paw Challenges." Here, a leader picked out a random kid from another youth group as prey for the Paw and commissioned one of our students to go for it. The surrounding youth groupers would all wait with bated breath to see if our student would follow through.

If they wanted clout, wanted to be entrusted with additional Panda Paw challenges, they would roll up to the unsuspecting victim, 3 finger salute their face, and walk back to us with head held high and the puff of victory in their chest.

It spread like wildfire across Daytona. There were more perplexed Panda Paw victims on the boardwalk than airbrushed tee shirts. Students could frequently be heard recounting their Panda Paw accounts and victory tales.

"I landed 8 today!"
"I got the concierge!"
"I'm not welcome back at Johnny Rockets!"

One student in particular stood out as our reigning champ.

He goes by Tiny Rock – and is every bit worthy of this caliber of nickname. At the time, Tiny Rock was a high school freshman with the personality and banter of a late night television host.

Witty. Smart. Quick. Willing. His hands were made to Paw.

When we needed a heavy hitter, Tiny Rock was the one we called. Until one time, when nerves and general civility got the best of him.

We were on break at the conference, and I had taken a crew of students back to the hotel to grab some things for the beach. Turning the corner in the hotel lobby, time turned slow-mo and an epic Super Hero soundtrack began playing in my head as the Panda Paw opps of all Panda Paw opps walked toward us.

I have heard providence is preparation meeting opportunity. And this day, this time, providence was leaving the hotel gym and trying not to be too noticed by the students swarming about, all too eager to notice him.

Providence was BigStuf worship leader, Phil Wickham.

The students loved him and the thought we were even staying in the same hotel was enough to make them giddy.

My eyes got big with the golden egg before us. I reached for Tiny Rock like a commanding officer unrolling an emergency action plan. It was go time.

"Panda Paw Challenge!" I said excitedly and gave my nod.

He saw Phil, and his eyes started wrestling. The want. The opportunity. The "Could I? Should I?" And then, the hesitation.

"You were born for this moment, Tiny Rock! This is your golden ticket, and I am Grandpa Joe and you are the candy man who can! Now, Panda Paw that pristine Phil Wickham face!!"

He took a step in Phil's direction. His 3 fingers snapped to attention, his arm shakily raised, as we waited to see if he would go through with it.

But Phil made uneasy eye contact and walked speedily on by. Tiny turned to me like a whipped puppy and whimpered, "I can't," as the opportunity that could have cemented his place in youth group folklore, boarded the elevator.

In a hilarious proclamation I can still hear booming through the hotel lobby, Tiny Rock whaled:

"WHO WOULD PANDA PAW PHIL WICKHAM??"

A youth group catchphrase was born, along with ample occasion for ridicule as the leaders (lovingly) berated him.

"Phil Wickham...he was right there..." we'd say as we passed Tiny, shaking our head in dissatisfaction. "To whom much is given..."

The missed Paw-sibility ate at him, and he declared he would not back down again.

We had heard from another student that Phil was staying on the 4th floor of the hotel. I did not know how reliable this intelligence was, but Tiny spent his spare moments thereafter camping out on the 4th floor, just in case providence knocked twice.

And it did. But not with Phil Wickham.

Our last day in Daytona, I walked down the sidewalk headed to the conference center. From across the street, I heard this hysterically excited, "Whitney! WHITTTTTNEYYYYY!!!!"

I looked around, trying to find our students in the crowd, and I saw Tiny Rock's hands shooting up, waving in the air to get my attention. Through the muffled mix of city sounds, I made out his voice, hoarse from shouting.

"Panda...Paw...John...Mark...REDEMPTION!!!"

Trying to piece together what he was saying, I made my way toward the students, all barreling to get the story out and wanting desperately to clue me in on what had them so excited.

Tiny took the reins.

"Just now! In the elevator! The most amazing thing happened! I PANDA PAW'D JOHN MARK!!!"

"John Mark" was John Mark Comer, a pastor and Bible teacher and our premier speaker for the week.[13] As someone who had been beloved by the kids and featured on the big screen – if this was true, it was BIG TIME. Could a Christian Celeb Panda Paw have really come to our youth troop??

"We were all on the elevator," (perhaps from another attempt at scoping out the famed 4th floor), "when the doors opened and in walked John Mark. None of us said a word, and he gave us a polite grin and pushed the button. My heart raced. I felt the call of God on my life. Stepping forward, I said, 'John Mark. I am really sorry, but I have to do this.' And then, I Panda Paw'd him. I Panda Paw'd him real good."

"GET OUT!!" I shrieked.

"Oh yeah," Tiny recalled. "I just reached up and wiped my fingers down his baffled face. One of my fingers even got

caught on his lip a little – like this."
*cue finger caught on lip demonstration

I doubled over and wiped tears at the retelling of the story.

"How did he respond??" I asked.

"He just looked super weirded out and got out on the next floor that opened, even though I don't think it's where he was headed."

The reenactments started and did not stop. We hooped and hollered and celebrated and danced our way into the conference room – purely delighting in this Panda Paw redemption story. My laughter tank overflowed as we attended the next session.

These conferences are divided into big group time where we all learn and sit under the same teaching together and then private, personal time where we find stillness and solitude, and let the Lord cement privately what His word taught publicly. After this session, it was stillness time.

Quiet is a hard commodity when tending to the needs of students, so leaders are encouraged to capitalize on it, too.

I found my place on a hotel terrace, got comfy in a deck chair, looked out at the waves, and pulled my Bible and notebook from my bag. I tried to drown out the speakers blasting whatever summer jams played in the background, as a light breeze and the smell of sunscreen padded the solitude.

Pushing the salt water dried hair out of my face, I soaked in the first moments of alone time I had in Daytona. It did not stay comfortable and refreshing for long, because I was not really alone. This strange guilt joined me.

It crawled in my lap, waved its sticky hands in my face, planted its weight on my gut, and lurked into my thoughts. I had to pay attention to it. It was too close to ignore.

Its voice threaded condemnation in my head, throwing laughter back in my face like a painful grenade. Shame shrapnel dug into my skin and psyche.

"You are supposed to be a leader, and here you are at a student conference – a spiritual, Jesus centric conference – a time to dwell and learn and build the faith of students, and what have you done? Not stirred revelation in the hearts of the next generation. Not turned anyone's eyes on Jesus. Not set an example for passionately pursuing Christ. You have LAUGHED. You have Panda Paw'd. You have somewhat encouraged stalking Phil Wickham on the 4th floor. You have participated in a procession of dumb fun, which has nothing to do with holiness. You have turned this into an irreverent joke. God is so disappointed – He is disgusted – in you and your laughter."

That may sound harsh, but shame is harsh.

My heart felt sick. I tried to sift through the piercing prosecution for what was true – tearing at the threads stitching this narrative. Did I have a defense? Was God disgusted in our laughter? Was He ashamed of our Panda Paw'ing? Had He brought us to Daytona Beach for something so much more, and I was leading kids astray and away from the heart of the Father with the lesser thrill of fun?

It was true that when I thought back over the week the biggest thing I remembered was laughter.

We had worshiped. We had sat under excellent teaching. We had bought books and merch from the gift shop. But when I got home the next day and someone asked me about the time away, I would jump to stories not of big, spiritually seeming significance or large callings or miracle healings.

I would tell of laughing. I would tell of Beanie Drumstick.

Anytime I attend a conference, I experience this phenomenon where in the sea of people, there will be one person I run into all the time. In front of me in the Starbucks line. At the hotel pool. Sharing the water fountain. There will be one person I never really get to know, who I just see at every turn.

At BigStuf, it was Beanie Drumstick – thus named because:

1) I never learned his real name.
2) He always wore a saggy beanie on his head and a pair of drum sticks in his pocket.[14]

I pointed out to the kids I was having multiple Beanie Drumstick sightings a day, and they caught on and began reporting back to me their Beanie Drumstick sightings.

It became our live action "Where's Waldo?"

Throughout the conference, BigStuf featured inspirational stories of kids throughout the world. Videos and presentations would introduce these kids to us and make us feel like new friends who cared about one another – showcasing how giving our resources impacts real lives in real ways.

Generosity allows BigStuf to intervene and impact the lives of these students. These stories are a highlight of big group time. They are well done and well told.

One night, they read an emotional letter written from a boy they were going to help by bringing aid to his family. The emotion and empathy were thick in the room, and then they announced this young man would not just be introduced via video. He was actually in the room with us!

Applause erupted and the anticipation of getting to "meet" him from stage swept us to our feet.

A huge spotlight turned on in the dark auditorium, intended to reveal our new hero and heart's focal point. Except, there was a mistake, and the light got the wrong location.

Instead of landing on the letter writer, it landed on – you guessed it: BEANIE STINKIN DRUMSTICK.

Walking along a wall in the side of the auditorium back to his seat, he froze as the light pierced his eyes. He struck a pose that belonged in the lineup of Wing's *Band on the Run* album cover and tried waving off the light and attention.

Mistaking him as the boy of the letter, the arena continued to applaud until the roar of the crowd confusingly tinkered out as we realized he was not making his way to the main stage and looked instead like he wanted to bolt or throw up or do both at the same time.

Of course, our students felt touched by an angel.

"Beanie Drumstick!!" we all shouted and pointed and gave each other stunned high-fives.

Eventually, the lighting department located the correct boy in the crowd, ushered him on stage, and apologized for the mistake.

We continued to strike that Beanie McCartney pose along any solid surface the rest of the week – as several of our pictures would testify.

38

The whole thing made me laugh. A lot.

So, I would tell of laughing, and fun, and Christian Celeb Panda Paw'ing, and Beanie Drumsticking, and I did not know what that meant for my leadership, for my faith, and for God's opinion of me.

I sat there uncomfortably – trying to figure out what this called for.

Repentance? A vow to be somber the rest of the time? A formal apology to Beanie Drumstick, John Mark, Phil Wickham, pandas (they didn't ask to be involved in this), and anyone else adversely affected by my immaturity and parody of what a Christian student conference chaperone ought to be?

My stomach turned. I picked up my phone, opened a search bar, and typed:

What does God think of laughter?

I was nervous about the results and how they would make me feel. But I needed to know. Only truth unthreads the needle of shame, and really, that was what I searched for.

The page loaded. I scrolled through, looking for something reliable. A name I recognized. Doctrine I could vouch for. Something to either hammer in the guilt or carry it off.

An article written by Jon Acuff grabbed my attention. Jon is a very funny and talented communicator who had spoken at the conference that week. The article was titled, "Should Humor Matter to Christians?"[15]

I opened it like Gatorade after a run in the sun.

In it, he references Psalm 126:2.

"Our mouths were filled with laughter, and our tongues with songs of joy. Then it was said among the nations, "The Lord has done great things for them." (NIV)

Jon expounds.

"Then. That's the most powerful word in that verse. The laughter was not just some frivolous thing. The laughter was not folly. It was not jest. It was a sign that the Lord has done great things for them. In all our flailing about to show people the goodness of God, I fear sometimes we've lost the simplest way. To laugh. To be overjoyed. To be full of mirth. Should humor matter to Christians? It mattered to God, and that's good enough for me."

There on the hotel terrace, I became Dorothy stepping over from grayscale Kansas to technicolor Oz. Shame choked out, and light and hope poured in, brought to me by the Author of laughter.

It was like the Holy Spirit said, "Laughter. I am so glad you brought that up! What if the people of God were known for it? What if they were marked by it? What if joy is what you were associated with to a world that does not know Jesus? What if your laughter and stories and fun and humor drew them in and then, to its ultimate source?"

Of course, the laughter I am liberated to in Christ is not a laughter that hurts or demeans or excludes, but the laughter that heals and draws and delights. It is the laughter that points us toward what is good and lovely, given by a Heavenly Father who is good and lovely.

What if laughter was not coleslaw at all, but rich, vanilla ice cream brought out at meals to complement and sweeten it? What if God holds the scoop?

Ice cream is never necessary to a meal.[16] It is pure grace.

I was still mulling this over when quiet time ended, and it was time to get ready for the evening session – our final of the week. I left the terrace in the in-between place. I was Dorothy looking over my shoulder.

I wanted this verse to be brought to me by God himself, for my exact time and place, but I also did not want to take Scripture out of context or assume because I like something, that makes it true. I continued to wrestle, hoping for something to pin the match and declare a winner.

We filed into the arena as a group, choosing a tribute to sprint ahead of everyone else to spread towels, bandanas, drawstring backpacks, and any other manner of swag over the rows of seats we needed to be able to sit together (a classic youth group move).

We took our seats and belted out the high-energy songs we had come to love and would carry home as melodic souvenirs. We cheered on the emcees and listened to the offering totals and hit the beach ball back to the center section when it came our way and made light attempts at "The Wave."

When John Mark Comer was announced and took the stage to close out the conference, we cheered him on and reached for our Bibles and notebooks and shifted in our seats to get comfortable, preparing for the Word of God to fill the room and move our hearts.

We listened intently to his meaningful, ever timely message about following Jesus. How it will cost us much to follow Him. How it will cost us even more not to. I nodded my head and scribbled notes in the margins of my purple Duck-taped NIV.

And then he hit a point that took on particular interest.

Not having a transcript, I'll paraphrase.

"When it comes to following Jesus, I need to warn you. It will require you to be weird. There are going to be things Jesus asks you to do that will be weird to those around you. There will be things He asks you not to do that will be weird to those around you. It won't make sense. But don't fear the weird! Some of you are actually weird already. You know how I know? Because one of you, ahem...Panda Paw'd me in the elevator today."

If there was a time when, simultaneously, my eyes got bigger and my mouth fell open quicker, I don't know it.

Our group LOST IT. Whatever "it" is, we had no more.

Panda-monium took over.

We rose to our feet, raised the roof, laughed, and high-fived until our hands rang. As a youth group, this was our Publisher's Clearing House check. There was no doubt in that auditorium which youth group the Panda Paw'er belonged to.

And I laughed in fun with everyone else.

But my joy was different, springing from a deep, secret place. When I sat back down, I not only laughed because of what just happened. I humbly delighted in a confirmation no one else saw. I heard an ice cream truck, parking in my faith.

God had poured hot fudge and sprinkles on the newly dished doctrine of laughter and its goodness, sealing this theme in my heart and smile.

Could it be that our laughter evidences the great, unnecessary but jubilant things God has done for us? Could it be those who don't know Him would hear these stories and wonder at His goodness, His kind playfulness? Could it be that laughter could even be reverent and humor, holy? Could it be God is worshiped – and delights – when we participate? Is humor not only good and fun – but an apologetic?

I smiled the rest of the night. The night where ice cream was on tap, and I kept going back for refills.

I still do. I laugh a lot. But it is not just because something is funny, and it is not because of an enlarged sense of humor, and it is not because it's my personality or preference.

It is because God has done good things for me. He has given laughter, and He has given reason to laugh.

And that is paw-erful.

...

"There is a time for everything...
a time to weep and a time to laugh."
Ecclesiastes 3: 1a, 4a, NIV

When I was not with middle and high school students during my 20s, I was with other 20 Somethings. Creating spaces for 20 Somethings in the church to not feel alone and to have a place to go for friends and fun is one of my greatest desires.

As a result, I have helped facilitate different groups with that purpose. One of the most memorable met in an older house turned creative team office in Florida.

On Tuesday nights we would line Ikea couches and bean bags along the central room's walls, set out Pop Tarts, brew cheap coffee, forget cream and sugar (because I drink it black and am selfish and forget other people don't), and pack out a room where we never quite figured out how to run air conditioning, and the plumbing was spotty and not "seeker friendly."

I did not care about any of that. To me, it was a ministry palace. A sacred place. A table where we could always pull up another chair. I beamed when the door opened, because it meant someone else was going to sit with us.

Some of my favorite moments and most cherished friendships happened around that invisible table of camaraderie. I feel emotional just writing about it. Not the sad sort of emotion. The grateful sort.

Most Tuesdays, after Bible delving and discussion as a big group, we broke up for prayer in smaller groups. Guys would stay in the main room and be done in about 4 minutes before going outside for glow-in-the-dark Frisbee.

Girls would head to a backroom known affectionately as "the cry room," emerging an hour later, teary and exhausted.

One night, nestled in the cry room, a friend laid her throbbing heart bare. Her teenage brother had been killed in a car accident barely a year before, and she shared the pain as her family plodded day by day through unending loss. In this reality, all we could offer was stillness, silence, and commiseration.

I slowed my breathing and so badly wanted to get it right. For her to feel safe pouring out her heart, whatever was in it. To honor the bravery it took to "go there." To help carry the weight, even an ounce of it, by not offering answers but sharing in sorrow.

I prayed for that as she talked, trying to pull down secret strength from heaven in that room where heaviness loomed undeniable and necessary. There was a palpable ache and the pensive knowledge that the Lord was near the brokenhearted – even more near than the tears carving makeup lines on our cheeks.

And then, through the wall, from the main room, I heard the faint, airy sound of a Native American wooden flute, piping out "Amazing Grace."

No, it was not a hallucination or spiritual dream state. They weren't "special" Pop Tarts.

This was an actual flute, actually playing "Amazing Grace."

Aron, a devoted member of our 20 Somethings crew, had been getting in touch with his Cherokee ancestry in that season and had started bringing along said flute with him to group.

To look at him, you would not guess this is his heritage. Aron is…how do I say…white. Very white to the eye.

Looking back, we didn't offer explanations to newbies as to why an Anglo member of our group sat peace pipe style on a bean bag in the corner of the room noodling on a flute. We just let it happen.

And it came in handy – like the night we learned it was someone's birthday.

"Aron, play 'Happy Birthday' and we'll all sing!" – I excitedly urged him, anxious to incorporate this unique feature of our group, like woodwind karaoke.

"I would," he said, "but I only know 'Amazing Grace.'" That he did, and we instead attempted to sing "Happy Birthday" to the tune of "Amazing Grace" – which I assure you, is a train wreck and completely ridiculous and one of my favorite things.

Now here we are on another night, in the cry room – where the familiar tune crashes into a sea of heartache, like a child unknowingly interrupting a serious, grown-up conversation.

In the midst of our tears, no one could act like this unorthodox serenade on the other side of the wall was not happening – though at first, we tried.

Eventually, someone snorted, tipping our giggle canoes, and dumping us into laughter's waters. We went overboard and splashed around together.

We all laughed. Like, really, really laughed. Like, we could laugh real laughs, while crying real tears.

"This is such a picture of life," I thought, smiling and tasting the saltwater on my lips. I locked in the moment, because I wanted to remember it always.

It seemed so simple and so clear that in the home of life, there are real rooms for crying – with real reasons to hurt, to wail, to mourn.

46

And on the other side of those walls, there are real rooms
for laughter – with real reasons to snort, to smile, to sing.

They can both be true at the same time. We can go back and
forth between rooms, not having to deny the reality of the other.

Whatever room we are in, the Lord is there –
more near than the laughter or tears.

Sara Groves sings an amazing song called
"In the Girl There's a Room."[17]

In it she sings about the complexities of life and soul.

The undeniable, fractured realities that break our hearts and
remind us of what is wrong in the world.

"And still," she sings, *"there are songs."*

The pain of life is undeniable.
The songs of life are undeniable, too.

Even in the cry rooms, I can hear them.

Songs that sound like a Native American wooden flute
bleeding through the wall, with a chorus of friends singing
"Happy Birthday" to the tune of "Amazing Grace."

It still makes me laugh.

Because the doctrine of laughter still sounds amazingly
grace-full.

Chapter Four
Mary in the Middle

Remember as a child how there were plenty of things you would be fine with getting for Christmas, but there was that one thing on the Christmas list that was the diamond among rhinestones?

The "one thing" gift. To get it meant everything, and to not get it, meant everything else was a disappointment.

I remember.

Teddy Ruxpin when I was 5.
My Size Barbie when I was 7.
An American Girl Doll when I was 9.[18]
Lime green Airwalks when I was 11.
Backstreet Boys anything when I was 13…or 31.

Ahh, the one things.

There were other toys and novelties and boy bands, of course, but these were the heavy hitters. These were the red jewel of Abu's eyes in the Cave of Wonders. Every package opened was really just a quest to see if it was the "one thing."

My one things changed when I got older.

No longer material or confined to Christmas, they had become "one thing" hopes for life. They couldn't be marked in a JC Penney catalogue with dog-eared pages for me to conveniently leave behind for grown-ups to find. These weren't gifts for grown-ups to buy.

These were gifts only a Heavenly Father could give.

And God does not have a catalogue. We don't get to flip through, ask Him his spending limit, compile a list, and be pretty sure that so long as our requests are within the allowance, they will be granted, like I always could with my Grandma.

I wanted to believe these one thing hopes on the list were promised – so long as they were written with a pure heart and the best of intentions. I wanted to look through Grandma God's closets and see if I could find them purchased and hidden, just waiting for a surprise holiday morning, when the promise paper would be torn off and lo and behold, the one thing would be mine.

50

His handwriting, placed on a package just the shape I had hoped for, would be evident, as would my excitement.

To: Whitney.

I received your list. Enjoy your one things!

XOXO – God

P.S. My favorite band is Backstreet Boys, too!

But as you might remember from real life Christmas snooping, we aren't always getting what was hoped for.

Faith is learning to trust the giver even when the closet looks bare, when the bag is emptied of its contents, and there is no diamond in sight.

...

I do not know if I can say I have a favorite Bible story, but a favorite among favorites is the death and resurrection of Lazarus recorded in John 11.

There are a thousand stories in this one story. With the many angles, characters, emotions, and truths, I have probably referenced the story of Lazarus more when talking about Jesus than any other.

I love what we learn about Him through it.

During my 20s, in the midst of a stinging "one thing" withheld, I needed what we learn about Him through a supporting cast member in it.

Mary. I had met Mary before.

At least, the one I call Mary in the Beginning.

This is the Mary given in Luke 10 as the Biblical picture of what a lover and listener of Jesus is. Mary in the Beginning abides at His feet, renowned for her humble and eager posture before the Lord. Meanwhile, her sister Martha is reprimanded for being busy and bustling with Jesus in the house.

Martha. The unflattering, unapproved Facebook photo we would burn down the internet to avoid.

Her sister Mary. The primly lit, favorably angled profile pic for which we strive.

Yes, I knew Mary in the Beginning – the Mary with a sturdy confidence in Christ's love and devotion to her and hers to Him.

Mary in the Beginning, who had always been so Biblically photogenic – like her counterpart, Mary in the End.

Mary in the End is the Mary who falls at Jesus' feet in adoration and gratitude. The Mary who attests to a miracle – who witnessed someone so precious to her raise back to life, only by the might and greatness of Jesus when her own abilities offered no help or hope in the situation, and she knew it.

The Mary who could only respond to what she'd seen and heard by pouring out her perfume and her life to the Lord she loves, the Jesus she follows, the God she believes in.

Mary in the End bears the evidence of Jesus' real and good and great grace in her life.

But there is another Mary. I call her Mary in the Middle.

And this is the Mary I'm abundantly grateful wasn't "untagged" from a moment she would hardly have wanted blasted to the multitudes in the midst of her pain and suffering and grief and disappointment.

This is the Mary who sends a letter to Jesus, asking for a diamond – knowing He can afford it, knowing it is in His budget, knowing He could easily mine it from His almighty power and holy compassion.

Mary had a "one thing." That her sick brother be healed. The brother Jesus loved. The brother she loved.

He had healed so many around them. A day's walk. A sincere request. Did she even question when sending whether or not He would respond? We have no way of knowing, but I don't think so.

I think her love logic then wouldn't be altogether different from our love logic now.

Jesus loves me. Jesus can do this.
I love Him. I want Him to do this.
He will do this.

Signed. Sealed. Delivered.
It's His now and mine soon.

Mary in the Middle. This is the Mary who kept one eye on the door and the other on her brother's labored breathing. This is the Mary holding off grief with hope – believing hope will finish what it starts.

This is the Mary putting faith in a miracle she believed would walk into the room before death did – with a diamond.

"Hang on, Lazarus. Our Lord is coming," I imagine her repeating to herself as she paced the room, beckoning the invisible plea to have a visible result.

And this is the Mary who watched her brother die and the diamond turn to dust. Tears drowning her eyes. Loss burning in her throat. Betrayed by hope and confused by the story, when the storyteller is nowhere to be seen and too late to make a difference.

This is the Mary trying to balance a real love for and faith in Jesus, with a raw disappointment in Him.

Mary in the Middle.

I was not at all expecting to meet her. Pain can become a doorway for all kinds of introductions. But this particular year, the year we met, was not supposed to be a year of pain.

This was to be a year of promise.

Not the sort of promise where agreements are made and hands are shaken. Not the sort of promise where I can look at the one who didn't hold up the bargain and say, "But you *SAID* ...", because it's not the sort of promise that is said aloud or guaranteed.

It was the sort of promise love logic drew up in my mind and hope collateral'd in my heart. It was the sort of promise that believed it saw diamond shaped packages in God's closet and imagined my name on the tags.

It was the sort of promise that scared me to think about not receiving, because I didn't want to live through the spiritual fallout if I didn't.

It was the sort of promise comfort alibi'd with, "Of course this will happen and then you'll never have to know what it's like to live without it! You wouldn't ask God for a dream and He gift a disappointment."

Love logic. Kid Christmas theology. Grandma God mentality. They crafted my list, checked it twice, and became the threads of my deepest prayers.

The year of the answers to the deepest prayers.

That is what this year was going to be. I felt it. The answers, the promise, the diamonds. They were breaking through, bubbling up, like underground streams waiting to flood the dry, tilled advent ground with hope and beauty.

I took note of all the signs and assurances this was not imagined. That hope was not mirage'ing me – and I would be diving in streams and swimming in dreams soon. Diamonds were dawning. They were a day's walk away.

But as quick as they surfaced, they went back down.

Swallowed up by the earth without explanation. Like the sunrise after a long night showed the top of its warm arc, painting the sky with the deep purples and rich golds of its palette to signal the start of a new thing – a "one thing" – and then disappeared, "JK" style, taking my hope and heart down with it.

It was like thinking I was waking up on Christmas morning but somehow the calendar glitched, and it's January, and nobody else knows the promised week got skipped, and it's just cold and dark and diamond-less.

January has much of the look of Christmas with none of the promise. I did not want to live through another January.

I had no idea what to do with all my letters asking for these diamonds when there was now, no Christmas in sight. I had no idea what to do with the embarrassment of getting the dawn wrong. I had no idea what to do with the deep disappointment attaching itself to all of me, in this haunting, heartbreaking January.

Heaviest still, I had no idea what to do with God.

The maker of the sunrise. The miner of diamonds.
The Father of Christmas. And now, the Lord of January.

Do you know what I noticed about Mary in the Middle that I had always missed before?

She did not know what to do with January either.

Right after her one thing was withheld and her cold, calloused January began, Jesus came. Martha went to Him and poured out her grief-stricken heart. In January, some people are Christmas confronters.

I am not, and I relate to Mary's non-confrontational, "new year, no Christmas" reaction.

She stayed behind. She did not run to Him. She did not throw herself into His arms. She allowed the house to cover her and put a barrier between her grief and what could have stopped the grief but came late.

Maybe it was because she was waiting to craft a logical conclusion to how this level of disappointment was reconcilable with a God of hope. Maybe it was because she needed a moment to compose and hide her thick loss under a veneer of faith.

Or maybe it was because she was not sure what to do with Jesus in January.

I see her in the house, her posture and pain saying, *"I still love you, Lord. I still believe in you. But I don't know that I'm ready to see you yet."*

Maybe Jesus would forget she was there, and she could just see Him again when she could fake it until she could make it, and the loss could be shrouded by a "mature" faith.

Haven't we all been there?

Sucking in our tears. Powdering our face. Hiding puffy eyes. Reaching for our shroud. Waiting for how we want to feel to match how we actually feel. Shoving our messy faith memorabilia under the bed and in the closets when we think the Lord is coming, so we don't have to see Him walk in and discover we've had loss, and we are upset, and we do not understand.

Surely false faith would make a better air freshener than the scent of our uncovered tears and pain.

But Jesus is not surprised by loss or afraid of cold. A shroud does not fool him. He will step right into our January. He will not ignore our fractured hearts. He will not look away from our loss. He will call for us when the house isn't clean, and the chaos hasn't made it to the closets.

He called for Mary by name, and Martha delivered the message.

"The Teacher is here and is calling for you."[19]

Mary went. Not because she suddenly understood why her brother was dead. Not because her heart pain miraculously left. Not because she found a covering big enough to contain her disappointment and mask her tears and thus, be presentable to God. She went, because the Teacher called.

Here in January, school was in session.

Faith classrooms just show up, uncomfortable and unannounced. They do not typically manifest when our pencils are sharpened and our notebooks are clean, and we've had our balanced breakfast and a cup of orange juice before smiling and waving goodbye to mom and stepping on the bus, ready and eager to learn in our pressed polos and new school shoes.

In this school, we do not get to pick our schedules – telling Guidance Counselor God what classes we would like to take, which we would like to avoid, how much homework we are comfortable with, and when we would like to complete our holiness degree so we can move on and join the faith workforce, having completed all our courses and learned all our lessons.

That is not how the Teacher works. He calls, and ready or not, we come. He calls, and whether we have bought school supplies or had breakfast or enrolled in this class or even put on shoes – we come. And He is never late for class.

Even if we thought He was scheduled for Christmas, and He arrives in January.

"Mary in the Middle?" He called.
"Present." She answered.

Mary brought her Christmas list, and with it, her heartache. Instead of hiding it, she showed it to the Teacher.

"Lord, if you had been here, my brother would not have died."[20]

I see her breath in the January air, escorting these words. Her lips blue and limbs quivering, accompanying the limited truth she's able to know this side of the miracle. I see the dust rising from the dry ground when she hits it, where the rain never came.

Jesus saw it, too. And the Holy Spirit helps me see something in Him. Here in January, warmth poured out of the Teacher.

A sun dawned – bigger and brighter than the hope that shrank back into the earth, shining on and surrounding her grief.

He does not reprimand her. He does not scoff at her pain or tell her how ashamed she should be at her lack of understanding. He does not bring out the red pen to circle all the ways she has failed in faith. He does not add to her humiliation or belittle her reaction to loss.

Do you know how He responded? How GOD responded to Mary in the Middle?

He wept.

God. Wildly weeping. Deeply moved. Spilling His tears on her dust. Joining her in her January.

This is our God.

He is not just the God of Marys in the Beginning and Marys in the End. He is the God of Marys in the Middle.

Marys waiting for a miracle. Marys unsure if they can face Him in disappointment. Marys fearing they will never know how to hope or trust or ask for a one thing again. Marys sitting in the dust at His feet, laying lifeless one things out, open-faced before Him, in the graveyard of the deepest prayers.

This is our Teacher.

He called me by name in my 20s. In my middle. In my loss.

I hit the dust at His feet, showing up with all my anger and grief and deep disappointment. I offered my, "Lord, if You had been here." I wept, because it was January when I wanted Christmas. I wept, because it was a loss I did not understand, a class I did not want to take, a graveyard I did not want to visit, a Christmas I did not want to skip, a hope I did not want to die, and a one thing I did not want delayed.

And He taught me – in the dust – that He is still Lord.

He is still warmth. He knows my name and sits with me in the disappointment until the miracle comes. He does not demand I front a "faith" that doesn't feel loss. He lets me be Mary in the Middle.

Spoiler alert: Mary's story does not end in the dust.

Lazarus' story does not end in death. Jesus called His name (powerful things happen when Jesus calls our name) and a "one thing" walked out of the tomb.

Because Jesus is who He is…

Januarys turn to Christmas.
Weeping turns to laughter.
Spring rains flood dusty classrooms.
Deepest prayers dance out of the grave.
Dead Lazarus' become living Lazarus'.

And sometimes we are Marys having to trust all of this in the middle, before we have reached the end.

I can't tell you the theme of my 20s has been that we always get what we want for Christmas and Christmas comes when we want it. That every dusty day ends in a miracle. That Marys in the Middle quickly and painlessly become Marys in the End after a letter and a few days.

But the dawning theme, written in broken pencil and carried around on dusty paper, has been that no story entrusted to Jesus ends in dust, graves, disappointment, or death.

The Teacher tells me so.

I can trust Him for miracles, for life in dark places, and with the deepest prayers – BUT the classrooms, the waiting rooms, will often be dusty and tearful.

Death precedes resurrection. Dust precedes diamonds. A dark winter may precede the Christmas He alone knows when to dawn.

As I wait, as I long, as I weep, as I do not understand, as I live in the daily advent that is new each morning and accords to an appointed calendar only He sees – the harshness of January tries to convince me the hope of Christmas doesn't exist.

"He is late," it taunts.
"Stay in the house," it says.
"Stop sending your letters," it shouts.

And I can listen to January, which calls Him names,
or I can listen to the Teacher, who calls my name.

He has not always changed the season when and how I want,
but He has – faithfully, lovingly – provided warmth in the cold.
He has been the fire I can sit beside, bringing color back to my
lips and calm to my quivering soul, no matter how long January
lasts and how cold the classroom gets and how I mourn the
one thing withheld.

The fire doesn't give answers. It does offer light in the mystery,
if I will sit beside it. In the light, I see my friend Mary.

I will join her in the dust every time I need to believe in a
miracle, every time I send a letter to the Teacher that feels
unanswered and ignored, and I want to drop the class.

I will keep coming when Jesus calls my name. I will know that
He is Lord, if I know nothing else. I will weep in His warmth.
I will call on His promises.

I won't wipe the dust off my knees, because I will remember the
dust is where I am best positioned to witness the miracle. It is
where I can be real with the Teacher. It is where I can wait for
the dawn.

As I wait, He waits with me. Mary in the Middle introduced me
to Jesus in my disappointment. When loss comes (and it will),
I know where to find her, and because of that, I know where to
find Him.

There.

In dust. In death. In disappointment.

When they come, He comes.

He calls. He teaches. He weeps. He speaks.

And He is never late.

"At just the right time…Christ died for the ungodly,"
Scripture teaches.[21]

At just the right time, He does everything else.

But when it feels like the wrong time, when it feels like the
too late time, when it is not the time I would like to be told…

He is the Christmas who warms me in January.
He is the dawn who sits with me in the dark.
He is the life that accompanies me to the graveyard.
He is the Teacher who weeps with His student.

He is the Beginning and the End who meets me in the middle.

Chapter Five
Grace Conspiracies

"The secret things belong to the Lord our God, but the things that are revealed belong to us and to our children forever, that we may follow all the words of this law."
– Deuteronomy 29:29, NIV

There are plenty of things in Scripture that are revealed.

I don't have to wonder if God is pro-gossip or how He wants me to treat my enemies. I don't need to labor over a definition of love or question what the fruit of the Spirit might look like.

I don't need to consult a spiritual heavy weight on if we are to be reconcilers or racists; humble or arrogant; generous or greedy; peace-making or prejudiced; merciful or merciless; honoring of one another or taking advantage of one other.

Because of Scripture, I know. It is not hidden.

Who does God consider blessed?
How am I to pray?
What do I do in relational conflict?

It is all there – revealed. Really, I lack nothing I need for daily obedience and faithfulness.

So, there are revealed things. For today.
And there are concealed things. For tomorrow.

"Future things are secret things."[22]

I read this line in a *Jesus Calling* devotional years ago, and if I have a corkboard soul, it earned a prime, thumbtack spot.

I love it, and I lament it, because I know it is true.

There are lots of things I want to know about the future and lots of secrets I want to be in on. But the secret things don't belong to me. They belong to the Lord. Faith means trusting they are better off that way.

…

I am naïve by nature.

I am just not the, *"I knew he was the bad guy the whole time!"* type. You will never hear me say it. If I do, I am most likely lying and trying to impress you. Do not believe me.

66

After the movie, I am the one cleaning popcorn off my shirt while my friends swap all their "Aha!" moments and hints and plot sleuthing and tellings of when obvious things became obvious things to them, which stayed un-obvious to me.

Twist endings always get me, I never figure out magic tricks, and I tap out early on any strategy-type game, because I flat do not pick up on things.

While this is a disadvantage for Settlers of Catan, sleight of hand, and M. Night Shyamalan movies, there is one area where a propensity for the oblivious remains a huge advantage.

Surprise parties. I am an easy target.

Three years in a row during my 20s, my friends threw me surprise parties, and I never caught on to one thing.

No picking up the scent when people randomly asked me about my favorite desserts, pizza toppings, or the contact info for my other friends they might need to get in touch with… near my birthday.

One of the most gracious nights of my life happened by surprise, right after I laid my first MacBook to rest.

It didn't die of natural causes. The coffee I dumped all over it at work one morning proved to be poison. Apparently, it didn't need the stuff like I do.

It left me in pieces, over time, like the caffeine had given it computer dementia. I had it with me for longer than I should have.

First, the trackpad went.

"No problem," I thought. *"I can USB that junk and have an extension mouse."*

Then the keyboard fizzled – starting with second-tier, luxury keys.

The exclamation point – *"I will just not be excited."*
The alt key – *"Who even knows what that is for?"*

But then the "E" tanked – *"Couldn't have been the tilde..."*
I can still hear my friend Mike say, attempting to fix it.

Then the question mark.

Until you have had to open an old Word document to copy and paste an "E" or an "?" when you need one, do you even know pain? Not to be dramatic, but it was the WORRRSSSSTTT.

I'd pound and poke that E with all the force my middle finger could muster, and every 1 out of 50 times, it cooperated, and I lived cussing under my breath and whining a lot. Eventually, I caved and started using an extension keyboard, too.

I found one in a tech graveyard closet in our office. It was huge and cumbersome. Coupled with the mouse, the ease of a laptop was gone, replaced by a Frankenstein, hodgepodge machine whose dangling cords I would get tangled up in and trip on anytime I carried it. I could legit play "Skip-It" (and did) with the dangling mouse's extra long cord, as it grazed the ground in transport.

My Mac had become the equivalent of what a true teenage car ought to be: mismatched, embarrassing, not entirely functional, something to pass on to a younger cousin for $20.

I was not a teenager anymore, so this did not embarrass me, and I could appreciate that my Mac had a character-factor, much more than a cool-factor.

I could deal, and deal I must. I do graphic design; therefore, my Mac is a pencil to a writer. It isn't just something used to check Twitter or store pictures. It directly affects my job.

So, the day it blinked off and never turned back on was not my most favorite day.

I kept "letting it rest," blowing one of those airhorn bazooka things into the keys, hoping for a Lazarus moment, hitting the power button to see if it would miraculously blink back.

It never did.

The computer guy at the emergency shop assured me it wouldn't either, as he told me the cost to fix it nearly matched the cost to buy a new one – nonchalantly, like I wasn't 26 and working at a church and had no extra four figures sitting around.

I had copied and pasted my last E. Goodbye, old Skip-It friend!

With no money set aside to replace it, I cried, questioned if I was too materialistic, and told myself I could share computers at work until I could save up enough for a new one.

The worst part, the part that made the tears sting, was knowing I had done this myself. Me and my stupid insistence on coffee in the morning without insistence on a lid. Me and my clumsy, arm swinging story-telling style with no regard for the deadly liquid in reach.

A $2 cup of coffee had taken out a $1500 investment, and it was my careless fault. And while I cried, a grace conspiracy began.

A couple weeks later, I was hosting a movie night. Not including me, there had been exactly 1 RSVP leading up to the event, because frankly, people didn't seem that interested, no matter how much I promoted there'd be pizza rolls.

Even my best friends didn't seem like they were coming and changed the subject when I brought it up. I tried not to push it and liked the math on approximately how many pizza rolls we'd each get.

Then, the unexpected. The day of, RSVPs poured in! I was excited but puzzled.

"Liz," I said to my friend, "you're not going to believe this, but all these people are coming tonight for the movie! Isn't that crazy? When I mentioned it last week, it seemed like no one was interested!"

Every time I checked my email there'd be two, three, four more RSVPs. As someone who loves to host events and get people together, an RSVP "Yes" is music to my soul, and I did a fun dance each time.

I got home from work and fired up the toaster oven. I took pillows off the bed and threw them onto the floor and brought in borrowed bean bags from my car to make seating room. People started arriving, and we packed it in.

When my living room is full of friends and friends-to-be, my heart is full. I sank into a bean bag with a smile and fired up the movie.

70

Ten minutes in, my friends asked me to stop it. They turned on the lights. I assumed there was a pizza roll down or someone had spilled a drink or we were about to play a game of, "Wait – where is that actor from??"

By the time I turned around from pausing the movie, all my friends stood in the back of the room, looking at me, smiley and expectant. I can still feel the tears spring into my eyes and the butterflies take flight in my stomach. I had no idea what was happening, but my gut knew it was special and purposeful.

"Whitney, we know your birthday is coming up,
and we want to surprise you with some things."

"Wait, what?" I kept saying. "This was a setup??
You all knew about this?" I tried to process.

My friend James who had also been trying to resurrect my Franken-Mac, stepped forward and gave me two boxes, wrapped in baby shower paper, because that was all they could find.

The packages did not contain a baby. The first had a fancy, hard-shell MacBook case – the kind I would have seen the price tag on at Best Buy and immediately passed up, heading for a cute, completely un-protective one at TJ Maxx.

The second package had an external hard drive.

"Oh no," I thought to myself, opening these gifts.
"They don't know my Mac is irreparable."

I thanked them and decided I would tuck these gifts away until I could save for a new laptop to use them with.

Then Olivia stepped forward with one more box.

Wouldn't you believe, it was the exact size, shape, and weight of a MacBook Pro. And wouldn't you even more believe holding it there in my living room, it still did not occur to me that was what it would be.

Because something so merciful doesn't occur to me.

What occurs to me is what is deserved, what is expected, what is earned. None of these applied.

Even as I tore off the first piece of paper and saw the Apple packaging, I asked if it was somehow my old one they had taken to refurbish and maybe they had gotten that air horn with the straw nozzle to work, and I had given up too soon.

"No, Whit. That is a brand new MacBook Pro."

I stared at it in awe, in wonder, in disbelief.

They knew they were giving me a gift. But holding my shiny new laptop, I knew what they were really giving me was a lesson on grace. They were really introducing me to a theme of how God works.

The Mac and its accessories were nice. Of course they were.

But what was in wrapping paper was not what I ultimately cared about or what humbled me to my core. The gifts themselves were great, but they were "stuff." They have an expiration date and will eventually end up in a landfill.

The heart, generosity, sacrifice, and friendship behind the gifts – those I will keep forever. Those have made a lasting, unfading impression that won't glitch, even if I could spill coffee on it.

"You would do this for me? You would go to this trouble? You would sacrifice, when I didn't deserve it? When I would have never known if you decided not to?" I kept saying it, thinking it, feeling it, over and over.

Standing in my living room, I went over what had to have happened for this conspiracy to unfold, as if it were a flash flood of memories I hadn't lived.

A Facebook event I wasn't invited to. Group chats explaining the situation. Invitations to be a part of the plan. Parking lot meetings to collect money. Best Buy trips. Day-of wrapping. Last minute preparations and whispers of, "Did you grab the hard drive or should I?" and "Hush, she's coming into the room!" and "We should probably spring for the warranty, right?"

And I had known NONE of it. All this happened behind the scenes. For me and not known by me. In the secret.

Grace didn't RSVP, but it was coming to the party.

I saw the Gospel in that crumpled baby shower wrapping paper hitting the floor. What is the Lord doing – what is He wrapping – behind the scenes, out of sight, when I accuse Him of not working?

As far as I knew, I was going to be watching a movie – hoping a couple people showed up and the pizza rolls cooked all the way and I didn't set the potholder on fire while retrieving them from the toaster oven because I am talking and not paying attention, like the last time.

The reality was far beyond what I knew.

How much preparation goes into gifts we don't see? How many times do we assume God isn't doing something because we don't see Him doing it?

When we feel forgotten. When we feel shutout. When we base reality solely on what we experience in our scene, forgetting all the scenes beyond our reach and out of our sight.

I still think about that night – like now, when I type this on that very Mac and the drink next to me is lid-locked.

I think about that mercy. I think about how quickly life can change and how God gives gifts in grace that take preparation. I think about how much preparation happens out of sight.

I think about how what we see happening is not a complete indicator of what is actually happening. And the next time I start to accuse, the next time I assume a lifetime of mundane movie nights, I remember surprise parties and hidden preparation.

Scripture says:

"No eye has seen, no ear has heard, no mind has imagined, what God has prepared for those who love him."
1 Corinthians 2:9, NLT

God prepares. And our eyes will not always see it. Our ears will not hear it. He works all things together for the grace receiver, independent of our knowledge and input.

I didn't wake up the morning of the movie night feeling like later that day I would be getting a massive surprise and one of the most generous gifts I have ever received.

That had nothing to do with whether or not that would happen.

The next time you feel forgotten, shutout, unable to face another day without change – remember the God who prepares, who crafts, who makes surprise parties out of mundane movie nights.

The next time your heart tells you to accuse God of not working on your behalf, of not caring in the way you feel you need – toss your assumptions out with the trash, throw some pizza rolls in the oven, and remember reality reaches far beyond what we see, hear, or imagine.

We can trust the preparer of the parties.

According to 1 Corinthians, He is not holding out on us.

He loves surprises.

Chapter Six
A Deep Note for Sticky Tables

*"Heaven is not here, it's there. If given all we wanted here,
our hearts would settle for this world rather than the next."*
– Elisabeth Elliot[23]

It is bitter cold out. The kind of cold that arrests you the
moment the car door opens. The kind of cold where you
realize 20 minutes into your stay at a restaurant you haven't
removed your coat, because you can't bear the thought.

The kind of cold where I spent valuable time with my dad combing our hometown looking for a heated dog bowl to keep Champ, our gigantic mutt's water from freezing before he can drink it.

We didn't find one. They were all sold out.

I am at the airport awaiting my flight back to Reno, where I currently live. It's New Years Day, and my makeup's all cried off. I know better than to wear contacts on a fly-back day, even though I generally avoid glasses in public.

Because I tend to wear them first thing in the morning, just before bed, or when I am sick, glasses make me feel like I am not yet ready for the day. They are appropriate today, because I am never ready for the day when I repack my suitcase, hug my family, and cry on my dad's Carhartt coat in the Southwest terminal.

He is too big for me to hug around the neck, so I hug his waist and he squeezes my shoulder and puts his chin on the top of my head. It is the safest, most secure hug I know.

Even though I have lived away most of my 20s – the airport scene never gets easier. On the drive to the St. Louis airport, through the farmlands of southern Illinois, I start choking up at our first stop, where Dad gases up the truck and brings me out a styrofoam cup of coffee. Sixty miles later the Arch breaks the skyline, announcing another trip home is over, and my heavy heart spills onto my cheeks. I am not a dainty crier, and I have no ability to sop up my tears before they come.

Dad parks his white Chevy in the cold airport parking garage and asks me to open my door and make sure we are in the lines. We are, so I step out while he unloads my suitcase from the tailgate, and I look for a terminal sign.

Airports, traffic, cities, sadness – they all make him nervous, so this mix is not his favorite. It is not mine either.

I clamp down on the button that unleashes the handle to roll my bag along the concrete and shiver as I walk, verbalizing how much I hate the cold, as if it will listen and excuse itself.

"Why don't you let me roll that?" Dad says, reaching for my luggage.

I hand it over, taking advantage of my last moments of having a dad present to do things like drive me to the airport, buy my coffee, have cough drops available in the console, and be in charge of my suitcase.

Walking without that weight behind me, hearing the wheels shift ownership and rattle and roll in hands not my own, my load feels instantly lighter, and my soul cannot help but bring up a parallel. As if the Holy Spirit came up strolling with us, through the dark garage and hard reality, saying, "Isn't that something?"

It is so much lighter when I am not carrying the baggage, and I can just walk next to my father as he rolls it.

I trust him with it. I am grateful not to hold it.

In a moment, I want to do the same with all my heart, future, hope, and fear. I want to walk next to my Heavenly Father into this new year, and let Him roll what is mine but what does not have to be mine to carry.

A simple picture. A cold frame on a sad day. Going home without the weight.

It is a last Christmas gift from the Lord himself.

I do not remember what we were talking about or what led into it, but along one of those sixty miles to the airport, Dad said, "I think we are not told much about heaven, because if we really knew what it was like, we could not stand to be here a moment longer. Most people forget this isn't heaven yet."

Most people forget this isn't heaven yet.

It is easy to forget, even though it seems like any look around would make it obvious.

I do not want to forget it anymore. I want to live both knowing the Kingdom of God is in our midst[24] and Jesus has gone to prepare a place for those who love Him.[25] In that place, God himself will be with us, wiping every tear from our eyes. Death and mourning and crying and pain will be no more, because the former things will have passed away.[26]

In our current reality, we still live amongst the former things. This is not heaven yet.

...

While home, I had breakfast with my cousin Kendra who is pregnant. Of course, it is exciting, but not the full package of excitement she envisioned growing up, dreaming of being a mother.

She wanted this pregnancy to be different. She wanted it several years earlier. She wanted it to not come following years of infertility, watching friends post happy birth announcements on their Facebook pages and Christmas cards, while she silently wept, wondering why it seemed so easy for them.

She wanted it to not come following a devastating miscarriage.

She wanted it to not follow the burial of a baby in the yard of her new Tennessee home she and her husband bought with visions of filling with a family. She wanted it to not happen after planting Forget Me Nots in memoriam to a child she would not get to know or hold or feed or cuddle.

She wanted a pregnancy full of joy and void of fear attached to it from having a pregnancy end earlier the same year.

To carry both excitement and grief is hard. It feels confusing and heavy and messy.

Her heart is both full and broken.

And what can I say to her, sitting across the booth, pouring syrup on my cinnamon pancakes, nodding yes to another coffee refill from the waitress? What can I offer this level of heartbreak?

I cannot say anything that makes sense. I would be a fool to try.

Because I do not know why miscarriages happen. I do not know why for some couples, having babies is as easy as ordering a pizza and for others, it is a haunting chase of wait and disappointment.

There are lots of other things I do not know about or attempt to explain or justify.

Hurricanes. Racism. Hunger. Poverty. Sex trafficking. Slavery. Exploitation. Deformities. Cancer. Judicial discrimination.

Why kids make fun of other kids on the playground.
Why I have made fun of other kids on the playground.

Injustice stings. Loss hurts. They breed questions. Weighty, burdensome questions that cut your mouth as you say them, because they are sharp and real.

And no matter how real they are, there is a reality deeper still, that melodizes underneath while I sit in that booth.

A steady, strong song – a solid note – full and trustworthy under the dissonant questions. Salve to the cuts, latching to my soul like spilled syrup to my hoodie sleeve on this sticky table.

This is what it says. This is what it sings.

No matter how harrowing the questions and how big the loss, there's not a single one that reverses the resurrection of Jesus.

When there is something I do not understand. When I try to comfort a friend whose heart has been broken from losing a baby. When I watch disease steal life from people I love. When I stare into the face of a mom whose daughter has been abused, and they live picking up the pieces. When I hear stories of racism and hatred. When evil signs its name to another headline.

I run to the tomb of Jesus. That is where the note is played. I keep it continually in my heart. There I can run alongside it and look inside the grave, and see He is not there. The grave's emptiness reminds me: He is exactly who He says He is, and there are big, hopeful, beautiful implications because of it.

This is not a book about why God allows painful things.

There are much better resources out there for that – written by much more scholarly, learned, eloquent, experienced people than me. I recommend reading them.[27]

I also recommend – when the reality is so painfully obvious – remembering this is not heaven yet. For those who put their trust in Jesus, we are headed there.

This is not the fanciful hope of a dreamer. This is the promise of the death defier. Let the one who walked out of His own tomb carry the questions.

No one and nothing else can.

...

Recently I heard a public figure say, "Why do we have to wait for another life for heaven? I am going to live as if heaven is now."

The context made it seem like anyone who looks forward to another world, another life beyond this one, is wasting time. The thought was well applauded on social media and many agreed from their keyboards.

I get the sentiment. Really, I do. I can see why someone who does not believe in Jesus or life after death thinks it is ridiculous to fixate on another world beyond this one.

Scripture teaches we are to bring the Kingdom of God to earth through the justice, love, mercy, forgiveness, sacrifice, compassion, and generosity of Christ. Believing in eternal life with God in a new heaven and a new earth is not an excuse to tap out and not make a difference in this one.

But, if I choose to live like this is it, to embrace the mantra of the public figure – that this is as good as it is gonna get, that this is the finale and the only heaven we will ever know – then what hope is there for my cousin?

Can I say to someone who is grieving, who has lost, who has wept until their strength is gone and their face is raw, who has built a shadowbox for a baby they never knew, who has watched their entire community flattened by a hurricane, who has heard the devastating diagnosis, who has experienced the effects of hate and murder and abuse…that this is heaven?

No. I cannot. Because, it is not. Every darkness, injustice, loss, and Forget Me Not reminds me of it.

And if I humble myself and renew my mind and listen for the deep note, they can also remind me of the One who promises another place. Who left a tomb behind to say death and loss do not end the story. Only He does.

We have a Father who does not have to leave at the airport. Who boards the plane with us and ensures the next destination. Who is trustworthy with the luggage. Who comes alongside, to carry every pain we hand over, saying, "Why don't you let me roll that, until we get there?"

I want to let Him carry it.

Every question. Every heartache. Every Forget Me Not.

It is not an issue of whether you and I will have questions and pain to hand over. Live in this world, and we will. We all will.

Because this is not heaven.

Yet.

Chapter Seven
Really, France?

I think we all have that friend who thinks what everyone else is thinking but isn't scared to say it. If you don't, I hope you'll get one. They make life much more fun.

I will not be that friend for you. My voice shakes and my lips quiver when I have to say something truthful but unpopular. I will spend more time telling you what I do not mean to say than what I actually mean to say. It is annoying. I am annoyed talking about it.

So, I am not that friend, but I have one.

Her name is Olivia.

She is brass tacks. She is real and really funny. The friend who makes you snort repeatedly and laugh through the night. She is who you want to go on vacation with.

So is our friend Liz.

As much as you need an Olivia friend, you need a Liz friend. She is the one who organizes your trips on a color-coded grid. She is the itinerizer. She is the "just give me your money and preferences, and I will make it happen" friend.

The research. The airfare. The Airbnb. The daily schedules. She manages all this while being laid back, cool, and fun. When we travel together, she handles it all, I handle it none, and I am so grateful for her.

Some of my favorite days have been in New York City with Olivia and Liz, where New York is all the things it's supposed to be. Loud. Chaotic. Busy. Bagel'y.

I love it.

On our first trip there, Liz packed our days full of museums, Broadway, Central Park, "Best of" lists, and places where we might run into Jimmy Fallon. We left our apartment before the sun came up and got back when it was due up again soon.

We learned that $6 Aeropostale moccasins were not the best choice for 15 mile days;[28] that the *Seinfeld* diner was every bit the tourist trap we were warned it would be; and that you can't just show up to Madison Square Garden the night of a Knicks game and expect to get tickets that cost less than a paycheck.

The trip had plenty of off-the-beaten-path'ness. Like a piano dive bar where there was nowhere to sit – not because it was full, but because there was literally no seating – and the duo providing music played a track mostly made up of bird noises.

It also had its fair shake of tourist attractions.

We wanted to experience everything.

The standard *Phantom of the Opera* performance.
Shake Shack. Wall Street. Times Square. A hotdog cart.
The TRL window. And of course, the Statue of Liberty.

"I can't believe I'm here!" I kept thinking as we walked into Battery Park, and I looked at the Manhattan skyline behind me. When you are a girl from the Midwest and live far, far away from anywhere that appears in movies, this is a frequent thought in mythical places like California and NYC.

Liz lead us to the edge of the harbor after a day of all the "Oohs!" and "Ahhhs!" the Big Apple had to offer and pulled back the curtain on the final stop of the day.

"There she is!" she proclaimed. We pulled our jackets closer in the fall breeze. "The Statue of Liberty!"

Ahh, the famed Statue of Liberty. The jewel of the Hudson. The exclamation point on New York's sentence. One of the most recognized and beloved landmarks of American history.

I squinted, staring out across the water, wondering what the proper response was for such a hallowed figure.

"Wow," I retorted, reaching for my phone for the obligatory tourist picture, silently wondering if my phone could zoom that much.

"Hmm." Olivia seemed confused.
"It's kind of a small guy, isn't it?"

We all thought it. She just said it.

And we threw back an obnoxious laughter cocktail brought about from lack of sleep, walking exhaustion, and funny truth, right there on the busy outlook stretch. We buckled to the gritty, concrete sidewalk and shook with laughter.

"REALLY, FRANCE?" she playfully ridiculed, making us roll all the more. "That's the best you could do?"

The thing no one tells you about the Statue of Liberty before you visit, is when you have spent a day walking amongst skyscrapers, it is just not that big. It is big in icon-status but relatively small out in the harbor.

Still.

When you see it, you are not supposed to say,
"Really, France?"

You are supposed to say, "How magnificent!" or "I have never felt more patriotic!" or "She's a beaut'."

You are supposed to put your hand over your heart, break out in "My Country Tis of Thee," and find something to salute.

You are not supposed to comment on how under-whelmed you are and cheekily imply France cheap-skated us.

But Olivia didn't care about that. She was honest. Our Statue of Liberty visit was much more memorable as a result.

...

88

Jesus had an Olivia named Thomas.

Thomas was the disciple who said what was on his mind and what was probably on everyone else's mind. One such scene took place in the final chapters of Jesus' life on earth.[29]

After sharing their last Passover meal together, Jesus took time to tell His disciples some valuable things. Some "you are going to need this when I am gone" level things. This was not talk of the weather or time for Yahtzee. This was listen-up stuff.

Jesus addressed that He would not be with them much longer, prompting Peter to ask, **"Lord, where are you going?"**

Jesus responded, **"Let not your hearts be troubled. Believe in God; believe also in me. In my Father's house are many rooms. If it were not so, would I have told you that I go to prepare a place for you? And if I go and prepare a place for you, I will come again and will take you to myself, that where I am you may be also. And you know the way to where I am going."**

Thomas responded, **"Lord, we do not know where you are going. How can we know the way?"**

In short:

Jesus: "I am not going to be here much longer."
Peter: "Where are you going?"
Jesus: "You know the way to where I am going."
Thomas: "Nope."

I was not there. I was not sitting in the room. I did not receive this news on a first-hand basis around that Passover meal.

But when I read this exchange, I picture Jesus pouring out that truth wine of, "You know the way to where I am going," and everyone else sipping along, nodding, like you are supposed to do when the teacher talks over your head or you are in a conversation with someone smarter than you, acting like you are on the same page – when really, you are not even sure you have the book.

I hear, "Uh huhs" and nervous eye contacts around the room, asking without asking, *"Do you know what He is talking about? Because I am just pretending to."*

Maybe there were Amens in agreement. Maybe there were internal searches for symbolism coupled with external facades of understanding.

But that is not Thomas. He looks in his cup. He does not understand what is in it, and he points out the obvious.

I see a hand shooting up after a pregnant pause.

"Lord, we do not know what You are talking about. We do not know the way to where You are going. You just said we did, but we do not. Maybe You think we are smarter than we are or maybe we need to think deeper or take another class or pay better attention. Maybe I was sick the day You told us, and I got behind. Whether or not I am supposed to get this, I do not. Please help."

Really, France?

Again, I was not there to know if Jesus smiled when giving His answer. That is just how I picture it.

Whether or not the Lord smiled – knowing Thomas' personality, his propensities, his "Really, France"ness – His response is one of my favorite moments in Scripture, because it captures much more than just this moment, this specific question, asked in this honest exchange.

It captures salvation.

If we search for salvation like a road trip destination – if our aim is the born again life, if our heart's GPS is set to God's Kingdom on earth, and if we are lost in finding it, Jesus is about to be the gas station attendant we find on a lonely highway.

He is about to give us directions to the road that sets us free. He is about to show us the way to get where we want to go, where God is, on the route paved by the truth and the Gospel.

And it is not conventional. It is not something you scribble on a scrap piece of paper with words like "Turn left" or "Keep going at the fork." It's not a route someone else is taking, so you can simply ride along.

Jesus spoke of a way and Thomas, recognizing He did not know what it was, wanted to know it.

"What is the way?" Thomas asked.
"I am the way," Jesus answered.

It is a curious answer. It is an unconventional way. It is like if instead of verbally giving you directions through pointing and gesturing and writing out steps, the gas station attendant takes your keys and gets in your car.

"But do you know the way?" you think in hesitation.

"I am the way."

He smiles, the engine revs, and you know this is going to be a different way than you have ever taken.

Many times in following Jesus, I have wanted to know the way. The Thomas way. The "give me easy directions, paint the picture, tell me the forecast, so I know how to pack" way. I want Him to show me the color-coded itinerary. Like Liz does.

That is not Jesus' way.

He is the way, and He reminds me all the time.

When I think about the future, it is a blank slate. I wonder how long I will live where I live. I wonder what people will come in and who will go out. I wonder if I will stay single or if someday, there will be a ring on my finger and kids in my home. I wonder if I will continue to enjoy good health or if my life will change with a diagnosis.

I agonize over decisions, thinking, *"What is the way to where God wants me to go? Will I find it? Will I miss it?"*

Like I am transported 2000 years to the Passover party, I hear afresh, "*I* am the way."

When my destination is set on the Father, Jesus is the way to every place I want to go.

Jesus is not a concrete direction. He is not a S.M.A.R.T goal. He is not a book on a shelf or video on YouTube.

He is the walking way. He is wisdom personified. He is living directions. That is not always comfortable.

Why would I think the way of the cross would be?

But He will take me where a roadmap never could.

I am the way. It is mystery, and it is grace. It is not dependent on a scholarly knowledge or an elitist benchmark of piety. It is not a secret code to crack or an email forward I may have missed.

I am the way. It is simple, and it is hard.

I am the way. Just like everything else about His life, it is not the way we would expect.

Following His way works itself out not in a sensationalized spectacle but in childlike trust. In daily faithfulness. In ordinary obedience. In the willingness to look foolish in the eyes of the world, because it is not from this world which we take our directions.

When I live in the way of Jesus, I forgive as He forgives. I love as He loves. I give as He gives. I make my aim pleasing the Father, being a great friend, making disciples, dying to myself.

I can do all of that without knowing the backdrop of my life in five years, and I can be freed from fear that I will make a wrong decision, that I will go the wrong way.

I am the way.

The way is in the driver's seat, and I do not worry myself with the details or if we are making good time or if that was the right turn.

I make my best effort in the power of the Holy Spirit to live in the way He lived and trust Him to get me where I am supposed to go.

I fuel with His word. I tune up with the wisdom of godly friends. I stay awake to the journey and pray continually.

Anyone who travels can testify: it is not the destination that makes the trip. It is who you go with. Give me exciting people and a boring destination over an exciting destination with boring people any day.

Maybe if Jesus had given us a roadmap to the Father, we would have taken off on our own, without Him. Slaves to the route. Too proud to ask for help. Captive to our own abilities and vehicles. Lost and alone. Bored out of our minds.

Instead of offering a roadmap, He becomes the road and vehicle Himself, and He invites us to ride along. To trust, to step in His direction, to toss Him the keys.

In Jesus, you do not have to know where you are going to know how you are getting there.

"But what is the way to where we are going?" your heart may ask still, because it is so foreign to every other way in life.

"I am the way," He still says and smiles and offers a seat in the car. Many times, that is as much as He will tell us.

The beauty is, it is as much as we need to know to get where He is taking us.

Chapter Eight
Only Love Remains

"And now these three remain: faith, hope and love.
But the greatest of these is love." – 1 Corinthians 13:13, NIV

When you follow the Lord and sow Scripture in your life, there will be times when a verse – that maybe you have heard one hundred times before – becomes new again.

Like the Bible suddenly became a pop-up book, and this verse reaches off the page, into your dimension. Like it is not made of ink and paper but life, breath, blood, and movement.

1 Corinthians 13 could be poetry. It is so beautiful.

You would not have to be a follower of Jesus to read it and recognize that. You would not have to be a Christian to have it read at your wedding or hung on a plaque in your kitchen.

The Holy Spirit took verse 13 of it down off the wall for me and hung it square in my conscience, as I stood in the back of a room I loved and knew I would not be back in.

The lights were dark, because we were watching a video. I was propped against the back wall coffee bar, too antsy to sit, as a room full of 20 Somethings sat in chairs arranged in semi-circles in front of me.

Two hours before I had gone to gather supplies from a storage closet and hit the floor, knees buckling, in jolting sobs. It was the first time I remember experiencing how physiological grief can be. How it can sneak up and steal control from our hands, taking the wheel and not asking where we want to go.

After letting it drive me for about ten minutes, I grabbed the wheel back, picked myself up, washed my face, and asked the Lord to please help me be as normal as possible.

"I'll be fine once people get here," I kept saying in my head.

It was a Wednesday, which had become synonymous with "Friends Day" in my heart, for this was the day 20 Somethings gathered on a corner of the church campus where I worked. We called this gathering ADVO, because our theme was to advocate for the name and ways of Jesus.

Our advocacy looked like four square and glow-in-the-dark Frisbee on a concrete slab, lit up by a tall pole light that buzzed and took time to fire up.

It smelled like coffee and two dozen Dunkin Donuts. It sounded like laughter and prayer circles and the nervous/brave voices of those learning the art of conversation with new people.

It felt like the time of my life.

I guess ADVO was a program, with enough structure to have a start time(ish) but not enough structure to feel too programmy.

It was a collage of worship nights, mini-messages, dodgeball tournaments, dance parties, onesie-attired events, trivia battles, and a strong love for 90s kids lore. (Think *All That* references and excuses to talk about Dunk-A-Roos...and a mandatory need to know everyone's BSB vs. N*Sync preference.)[30]

My Uncle Bret is a gifted communicator and pastor. He has a sermon series in his archives called *Made for This*, encouraging the people of God to know the mission of God and discover our personal mission within it.[31]

ADVO was my "made for this." I felt it every Wednesday-Friends Day. In fact, I had never felt as made for anything as I did for that place, with those people.

Pointing 20 Somethings to Jesus. Making the church not a Sunday morning activity but a community with names and faces and inside jokes and shared stories and mission. Merging spirituality and personality. Gathering for coffee and camaraderie.

Every week felt like a discipleship training camp. A place where following Jesus sprung from concept to real life.

This was where the Lord coached me on conversationally washing people's feet.

Where wisdom would whisper in my heart, *"Say something dumb and welcoming rather than not saying anything at all,"* as a new, nervous person approached.

It was where God taught me being welcoming mattered more than being cool or impressive. It was where the Lord showed me being friendly is a choice, not a personality type and every day, every interaction it is my choice to make.

Before group time, our leaders would circle up and remind each other that by next week, it was likely no one would remember what songs we played or what the message was about (humbling, as the person who generally delivered it) or how the coffee tasted or if their favorite donut was represented.

They would remember how they were treated. Our focus then every week, was to treat people well and care they were there.

We wanted to decide beforehand everyone who walked up was a friend waiting to happen, and we would treat them as such. Even when it was hard. Even when it was awkward. Even when it would be easier to continue talking to the people we already knew and stay where we were already comfortable.

I have never regretted pushing through the nerves and complacency to welcome someone. I have often regretted when I haven't.

If people decided not to come back because they didn't know how they felt about Jesus or the Bible or because they were offended by something we believe, I was fine with that. That was out of our control.

But it was our ambition if someone decided not to come back, it would have nothing to do with how they were treated.

Our goal was that someone could say, "I'm not sure how I feel about church, but dang, they are friendly, sincere, kind, and welcoming people."

We didn't get it right all the time. I know we didn't bat one thousand. But I do know we were swinging.

On this particular Wednesday, where I had sobbed on the supply closet floor, I knew it was our last ADVO but hardly anyone else did. A week before, I did not know. I knew now.

I am as indecisive a person as you will meet.

One time I stood in a grocery store for 15 minutes debating if I should buy *shaved* parmesan or *shredded* parmesan for a soup I made. I couldn't even call the friend who would normally help me navigate such tough cheese waters, because it was a surprise meal for her.

I still send pictures of clothes to my sister to see if I like them, and I will draft 20 near-duplicate designs for a project and pull people into my office who have no background or care for graphic design and ask, "Which one do you like?"

I will go up, down, and all around rather than make a call on something.

So, when the Lord made it clear it was time to leave the job I loved, the place I loved, the people I loved when I did not know what was next, when I knew there would be accusations I was doing the wrong thing and false pretense surrounding the story – and I had no indecision about it? None? Zero percent?

It was all I needed to know. It was the easiest hard decision I had ever made. Still, the implications throbbed.

One of the greatest myths in person-dom is that right decisions are painless decisions. To any of you in the middle of a decision you know is right but is hard, take heart and do not assume the heartache means you got it wrong. Peace is not always painless.

I had both peace and pain that night.

My mind cried in the back of the room, knowing when I poured the last of the coffee down the drain, I would not be back to refill it. Knowing when I turned the lock at the end of the night, I would not open it up again. Knowing when we bagged the trash to take to the dumpster on our way to our cars, this was the last time I would see the gang of raccoons on parade coming out of the shadows to pilfer our contributions as my friends and I rehashed the night under the stars, thanking God this was our life.

This was the last time I would be in this room with these people. This was the last time they would be in this room with each other.

I would always close the night by saying, "Hang out, have fun, and we will see you next week!" And this time, I knew I would leave out the last part.

There were a million questions I did not have answers to, and I flipped through all of them. With everyone else's attention on the screen in front, the Holy Spirit found me in the back of the room and leaned in for a conversation.

When I talk about "hearing from God," I do not mean audibly. I have never heard the voice of God like I have a voicemail.

It has been more of an impression. Like breath on glass.

Like a person whose form is invisible, but whose presence is not, breathes on a surface and leaves something that was not there before. That is why I think Scripture tells us to have a pure heart. A pure heart can hold the impression.

I have heard other disciples of Jesus describe it as when something drops into your mind, that you know is not from yourself. When it aligns with truth, when it echoes of God's written word, and when it is not your own voice. For me, it is more like words I feel rather than hear.

In not my own voice, I felt the words: *Do you see it now?*

"See what?" I wondered and stared at the shape left behind by these words.

Do you see it now, because you won't see it then.

I studied the impression.

Only love remains.

Did I see it now? It was straight out of 1 Corinthians 13 and straight into the room where I stood.

Here I was, about to close shop on a "made for this" in my life. About to give my last hugs and say my last encouragements and demonstrate my heart for the last time to people so dear to me, for a cause so dear to me.

And when it was done, when the doors closed, when the buzzing lights flickered off, when the last of the trash was bagged and heaved into the dumpster, and when the supply closet was packed away and its contents disposed – only love would remain.

How many times, I wondered, had I fixated on the wrong things. On the ceasing things. On if the words were all right. On if the couches were in proper position. On if that game was too cheesy or that icebreaker too lame.

And none of that would remain.

Any energy and effort put into being cool or memorable or impressive or something that could keep up and compare with the outside world – none of that, NONE of that, would remain.

I could see it now.

All the insistence felt over these precious years to be sincere in love and fervent in friendship – it had been a gracious gift from our Heavenly Father. He knew ultimately the surroundings were all temporary, and faith, hope, and love would be all that would remain – and the greatest of these would be love.

If we do not invest in love in whatever we do, there will be nothing that remains. The part that requires faith, the part that demands wisdom and prudence, is seeing that *now*. Investing in what remains before we have seen the product and payoff.

We do not get to go back and see it then.

I could not wind back the Wednesday clock and say, "Oh! I get it now! Let's do this all over and this time, focus on loving people well because when it is over, that is all we will care about! That is all that will remain when this no longer does!"

It does not work that way. We must see it now, because we do not get to go back and see it then.

Love is the investment we will never regret making, and it is always an investment we have the opportunity to make.

We live in a society that heralds the words and sentiments of love, but sometimes I wonder if we know what we are asking for when we call for it.

Because love is not lightweight. It is not something you post on a wall or wear on a tee shirt.

That same chapter of 1 Corinthians tells us exactly what love is.

Love is patience and kindness. Love is not envious or boastful. Love is never arrogant or rude. Love does not insist on its own way. Love is not irritable or resentful. Love does not rejoice at wrongdoing but rejoices with truth. Love bears all things, believes all things, hopes all things, endures all things. Love never ends. Love is what remains.

And if it were easy, we'd all be doing it.

Jesus, love personified, tells us what love is, and it is not a conjured feeling. It is a decision born of character, and it will be HARD.

Love will frustrate us, cost us, challenge us, shape us, transform us, and ultimately, save us from all the futile, worthless ways underneath it.

Love is not slapping "heart you!" at the end of the text message.

Love is being patient when you have explained how to do it twelve times already. It is being kind when you would rather avoid. It is cheering someone on rather than envying them. It is laying down the boast or brag before you make it. It is insisting on someone else's way rather than your own. It is purifying every word, action, and facial expression from irritation and resentment before putting it out into the atmosphere.

If someone describes you as a loving person, it will not be because you talked about love or agreed with the concept of love. It will be because you practiced love.

Love will not be the easy way or the natural way, but it will always be the way worth taking, and it alone produces what will remain.

Can you see it now? It will change what remains then.

The reason advocating for the name and ways of Jesus mattered so much to a pack of 20 Somethings in Sarasota, and must matter to every Jesus follower, is because as the children of God, love is all that distinguishes us from anything else on earth.

For those in Christ, we must hold love – real love, costly love, sacrificial love – as our greatest aim. It is what He has given us to give to others. It is what He wants us to be known for.

Jesus did not say Christians would be known for our good coffee and donuts. He did not say the world would recognize us for our quality entertainment and cool factor.

I am not saying we shouldn't serve coffee or we should settle for being lame in what we produce. I am saying instead, if that is our aim, if that is all we offer, we have merely offered what people can find in multiple venues all over town. That will never be distinct to us. If that is what we offer, we offer what no one is missing out on.

But to offer the name and ways of Jesus…

That is to offer mercy, sincere friendship, and hope. That is to offer soul reconciliation, with God and with one another. That is offering mission, meaning, and truth.

That is enduring in patience, kindness, and humility. That is becoming sacrificial love for the benefit of other people.

And that is rare. And that is distinctly Christian, because that is distinctly Christ.

Long after the coffee filters hit the trash and the donut leftovers are tossed to the raccoons, what is done for and in the way of Christ will be what remains.

Do you see it now?

Chapter Nine
Psalm 37 and How I Drive by Taco Bell Sometimes

"Delight yourself in the Lord and he will give you the desires of your heart. Commit your way to the Lord; trust in him and he will do this: He will make your righteousness shine like the dawn, the justice of your cause like the noonday sun."
– Psalm 37: 4-6, NIV

"I do not know. I am still trying to figure it out. Any thoughts?"

I consulted with Pastor Joe, the youth pastor on staff where I interned.

I called him Pastor Joe-da, both because he was wise and because he once hosted a Star Wars night for our small group. If the pun fits…

A few days before, I had been offered a full-time job at the church in Florida, and I needed to make a decision. It was a big decision.

Florida was far from home. This would be my first "big girl" job, and I feared getting it wrong.

I felt like I was in a dark room, arms out, hoping to bump into the Lord, so I could say, "There you are! Tell me what to do!"

I read my Bible for direction, asking the Holy Spirit to magically work in something like, "Love your neighbor as yourself. Also, take the job in Florida, Whitney."

That did not happen. I continued to pray, seek, read, and ask godly people for advice.

Joe loves the word of God. As much as anyone I know. He meditates on it. He knows it. He would be a first round pick in any Sword Drill draft; therefore, I wasn't surprised when his answer came from Scripture. I was surprised – and actually terrified – by the one he chose and way he approached it.

"Whitney, why don't you just do what you want?"

WHAT?? Did he hear what he just said? Wasn't that counter to my every Christian inclination? Wasn't what I want to do always a snare? A trap? An enemy? Didn't my wants need to be surfaced, killed, burned, and buried?

To just do what I wanted? How would I even do that?

My confused face begged for exegesis.

"Whitney, if you have prayed about this, if you have sought the Lord, if you have delighted yourself in Him, then do what you want! And it will be what He wants. That is trusting Psalm 37:4 and putting it into action."

The freedom I felt in that moment was largely liberating and a little suspect. Did my decision really hinge more on whether I had delighted in the Lord and less on my ability to uncover the divine field guide for my life?

As I walk with Jesus, sometimes in the most ordinary moments, it is like heaven tosses me a key, and says, "Add this to your existential key ring."

Each key is an accessible truth that will not tarnish, fade, or change. There in Pastor Joe's office was a key ring moment.

Delight yourself in the Lord, and then do what you want.

When it is time for a big decision in life, it is tempting to seek signs and look for clues.

"Is my pancake in the shape of Florida, so I am supposed to stay?"

"Was that an Illinois license plate on the car driving by, so I am supposed to go?"

In these days spent weighing the decision to stay or go, I had never asked what I wanted to do. I had not even thought of it.

Actually, my theology had been the opposite.

"If this is what I want, then it is probably wrong, so I should do what makes me feel most miserable. That would be godly and right, right?"

That key was cut in fear and self doubt and had nothing to do with truth or the Father's heart.

But *this* key, the one Pastor Joe-da handed me, was cut from the truth of Psalm 37. It differed from the one I had been using and felt foreign in my hand. I wondered if I wasn't an exception to it and if I was supposed to learn to use it.

The more I thought about Psalm 37, the more its key opened the "deepest wants" principle. Anyone who is friends with me has heard me talk about this.

We all have wants in life, and then, we have deeper wants.

I want to eat cookies every day of my life, in between every meal of my life. I want candy corn for breakfast. I want to never have to pump gas or get my oil changed again. I want to not bother with a budget when I get my paycheck. I want to overstay dry shampoo's welcome and not have to go through the tyranny of water washing my hair. I want to grocery shop and meal prep once and then never have to do it again. I want the benefits of running, without having to run. Some days, I want to stay in bed under my heated blanket and not work and not look decent and not have responsibility.

These are wants. But thankfully, I have deeper wants.

I want to avoid diabetes and cavities on the reg'. I want my car to work. I want to be wise with the money God has allowed me to earn. I want to take care of myself and look like a human and not have hair that smells like a foot and is gag-to-the-touch.

I want to eat healthy (some days). I want to be active and in some kind of shape. I want to be a good employee and honor those I work with and for.

It will be our deepest wants that win out. That is why it is so important – it is so key – to take the time to know what they are and abide by them. I think of it as the Taco Bell rule.

I wish it were only a metaphor. It is not. It is my real life.

I drive by a Taco Bell on my way home from work. Most every night, my cheesy gordita crunch loving flesh tries to convince me that it would be much easier and much better to just swing through and order food and not prepare a meal when I get home. The urge pulls at my steering wheel, as I fight to set my thoughts on things above and not commit Baja Blast-phemy on things below.

The ease, the trash food, the quick comfort –
that IS what I want in the moment.

But if I will dig deeper, if I get below the surface, if I abide in what is best, I arrive at what I really want for the long haul – even more than Nachos Bell Grande. Here is where I want to form healthy habits, save money when I can, and not have my car smell like a taco on wheels.

Here is where I fight the good fight, get myself home, and prepare nourishing food I have already bought.

When I drive by Taco Bell (*"Goodbye, my lovvveeee!!"*), it is not because I stopped wanting it. It is because I wanted something else *more*. It is because I am feeding the deeper wants and letting them drive me home.

...

The first time I wanted to have character more than I wanted to be funny is like a movie scene locked in my brain. It was pivotal proof Jesus was changing me from the inside out.

I was with a group of friends – funny people, all laughing and telling stories and joking.

A name came up. We did not see the name as representing an actual person. We saw it as a target to hurl comedy darts at, trying to impress each other with our wit and sharpness.
(At least, that is what I was trying to do.)

In the banter circle, I had something to throw. My mind picked up a quippy remark, but as my tongue went to launch it, it got caught in my throat, and I couldn't do it. I could not voice it.

Yes, whatever the insult was – it was funny. It was par for the rude course, but it was also hurtful. It was the kind of thing I would not have said had the person been in the room and would only be easy to say because the person was not, and the morality bar was low.

It was like I had eaten something and gotten joke poisoning instead of food poisoning. I wanted to throw up. Like I could finally taste these darts sitting in my mouth were poison.
I wanted to swallow them back down instead of putting them out into the air.

No one else in the room knew this was happening, but heaven met earth for me in that moment as the Spirit of God called me higher, hitting me with a heavy, transformational question.

Do you want to get cheap laughs or do you want to have character? What is your deeper want? Stop right here and decide.

And I knew my answer.

I knew in a way I had not known hundreds of times before when I thought saying something to make people laugh mattered more than anything. Judging by my actions and history, I certainly honored being funny more than I honored other people.

How foolish. Who even remembers those jokes by the next day? How often do they get credited to another person anyway?

How quickly I had been tempted to exchange integrity for a remark no one would remember tomorrow. Grace opened my eyes and busted the scam.

An extreme mouth makeover had begun in the place all major character makeovers begin: the heart. The house of my desires. My tongue would change as my desires changed and their home was remodeled.

Because I wanted to take following Jesus seriously in every area of my life (which very much includes how I use language), God grabbed my tongue and took me to school.

I entered a life-long course called, "Using Your Mouth to Encourage, Bless, and Build Up – and Not to Tear Down."

Having an emphasis on building up does not mean I never get to be funny or joke again. It means when the funny interferes with character or loving people well, I need to lay it down and walk away toward my deeper desire, where I want to represent Christ in how I speak more than I want a quick laugh.

Picture a heart having dumbwaiters.

In mine, the dumbwaiter born of delighting in the Lord finally gained more weight than the want to impress my friends – and I could step aboard and take it deeper to the heart of Jesus.

What are your weightiest wants? Delighting in the Lord will change them.

Delight yourself in the Lord, and the want to be funny at the expense of someone else will be eclipsed by the want to be compassionate.

Delight yourself in the Lord, and the want to state your case and be the "most right" person in the room will back down when facing the want to give the grace you have received and honor another person.

Delight yourself in the Lord, and the want to walk into territory you know can be dark and dangerous for your integrity will fall under the want to be pure hearted and blameless.

Delight yourself in the Lord, and the want to give up and cower will be decimated under the want to have courage and be faithful.

This Psalm 37 key changed my whole world and unlocked a thousand heavenly dumbwaiters.

It is not getting "the decision" right. It is getting my heart right, by putting the weight of grace in the right place. Joe knew it, and I needed to learn it.

Delight myself in the Lord and His wants become my wants, and I experience refining freedom and transforming grace.

114

Delight myself in the Lord and I have a reason to drive by the Taco Bells of life on my way home – where the better food is served.

Psalm 37 opened the door to stay in Florida. Years later, it opened the door to move to Nevada. It's where I live now and where I frequently walk the Sierra Nevada mountains near my house.

There is a "rugged"-ness to them. They are rocky and dusty and steep. They never feel easy, and I love them. I see so much beauty in them. They challenge me while taking me to views I cannot see from the ground. They are where I go to work out my wants.

On a day off, I laced my dusty shoes and headed out, my heart pent-up with fear and frustration that needed to air out in the way nature tends to do. Most often, my fears, like the air, thin with elevation.

I needed plenty of elevation this day, as I had another moving decision to make. This one was not a physical move but a move of the soul. It was another stay or go decision. Not one that required packing boxes or a moving truck but a move in deciding how I wanted to live.

There on the mountain, I was in a desires cage match.

In one corner, I confronted the desire to stay passive in hope.

Here, I could be complacent and call it patient; faithless and call it wise; live courage-lessly and call it waiting.

I had lived in this corner for some time and was comfortable here, where I never got knocked out, but I also never took a swing.

In the other corner was the desire to run toward what I hoped for. Even if I looked stupid. Even if it scared me. Even if I cramped up along the way or had to ask for directions or tripped and face planted.

Would the desire to run toward bravery be bigger than the desire for safety? I was scared of being uncomfortable and vulnerable – which the running required – but I was also scared of timidity and cowardice.

Did God want me to run toward my deepest wants? Did He care? Was He sitting in either corner? Could His desire for me not be a certain situational outcome or expectation but the character traits of trusting and leaping?

Do not read me wrong. Sometimes the bravest thing we can do is wait. Scripture has much to say about patience and waiting, and there will be times God leads us to do that.

And there will also be times He leads us to GO.

To run. To move. To risk.

In these times, when the light switches from red to green, we have the choice of saying, "No thanks! I'll catch the next one," in fear, or, "I don't know what is on the other side of that green – and it might be painful – but I am going," in faith.

There on the sagebrush hilltop in the Sierra Nevadas, I felt the light change, and I needed to turn the engine with the key first handed to me in Pastor Joe-da's office.

"What do I most want?" I looked at both corners.

Surely, it was more practical to stay in status quo corner and continue to be how I had been.

The possibility for pain through vulnerability? Please, no. How could that be what I want?

Anyone would understand why it is too dangerous to switch corners, Whit! Stay here. Stay comfy. Stay the same.

In my mind, this voice sounded a lot like fear (and also Mickey from the *Rocky* franchise, but that is because I have an older brother, and we watched a lot of Rocky over the years).

The other corner spoke, too – gently and with authority.

Whitney, maybe this time, you want to be bold, courageous, and faithful more than you want to avoid discomfort.

Hey, key. It was time to get up and go on green.

The deeper I delight in the Lord, the deeper my wants for the attributes of godliness win out over the lesser wants of comfort and cowardice.

When you have a decision to make, do not start with the decision. Start with delighting in the Lord. Then, when He is what you want, do what you want.

Cut the keys of your life from the wisdom, truth, and authority of Scripture and the heart of our Heavenly Father. They will not tarnish. They will not fail. They will not lose power.

They will lead you to your deepest wants.

And in my case, past Taco Bell…sometimes.

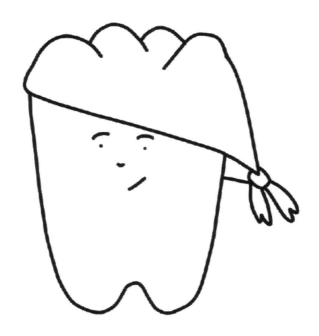

Chapter Ten
Intricately Woven: An Ode to Peppers

It was the classic story of the daughter's car being packed up and loaded down, ready to leave her parent's Midwestern driveway.

It was my Tom Petty song.

I had just graduated college in Indiana and the next stop was Sarasota, Florida for an internship at my uncle's church a thousand miles away.

When most people think of following the Lord and dying to themselves, they picture a remote village in a far off country without plumbing, electricity, drive-thrus, or wifi.

Sleeping under a mosquito net. Developing an immunity to unrefrigerated meat. Daily donning a missionary skirt and topknot. At least, that was what I pictured when I knew I would go into ministry.

When the first call after graduation came not from a foreign field but from a tropical, beachside town where my biggest struggle would not be malaria but keeping sand out of my floorboard? I was confused but went with it.

Still, it does not matter how cool or beachy or beautiful the destination is where you are headed. When you do not have friends or familiarity there, it will be hard to leave where you have all that.

The tears flowed as I power hugged my parents before loading the last thing into my Chevy Cobalt to leave – myself.

The driver side door was open, ringing out the annoying "ding…ding…ding…" indicator. Mosquitos wafted in, congregating at the dome light on this August night.

I could not speak. The three of us cried and embraced the goodbye. My dad tilted his head down and said one of the most influential phrases of my life to that point and beyond.

"You just be yourself, Whit, and everything will be fine."

It almost sounds too simple to be effective. At first glance, it may seem more cliché than pithy. But my dad doesn't speak in clichés. He speaks in truth. When he speaks, I listen.

There was a time that, had someone told me to "just be myself," I would have internally rolled my eyes. I would have thought, *"Well, yeah. What else am I going to be?"*

Aren't we always ourselves? Do we even have a choice?

Maturity and experience have revealed learning how to be ourselves is absolutely a choice and a game changing one.

"Be yourself" isn't the same as saying, "Have brown eyes, be born in September, like what you like – and everything will be fine."

It is not an out-of-our-control factor. It is a direction we step in.

It is a place we abide.

...

I have so many examples of having no idea who I was.

Sometimes I wish I could banish them from memory. Sometimes I am grateful for the laugh and the humility check. You probably have similar memories. For me, they can be identified with the word "phase."

I had a Tweety Bird phase at 9. An *I Love Lucy* phase at 13. An ultra embarrassing doo-rag phase freshman year. An "I hate name brands" phase the rest of high school. A "leggings every day" phase I am still in and will likely never come out of. #DeathToRealPants

What I see when I am sent a picture from a high school friend – taken on a disposable camera with horrible flash lighting and the caption "hahahahaha" – of me in a doo-rag; or when I find a box of Tweety Bird paraphernalia in my parent's storage shed;

or when I remember a ridiculous thing I said or tried to imitate, is a girl desperately wanting something to dictate who she was.

We all look for things outside of ourselves to tell us who we are.

If you are not sure if that is true, hang around some middle schoolers for a while. They want a group, they want a music style, they want a signature drink from Starbucks – maybe not even because they like those things, but because they want an identity.

"Just tell me what group I belong to – and then I will know how to dress, how to talk, how to walk, what to think, what I like, and what I don't. That would be so much easier than finding out who Christ has made me to be, and safer than if I discover that person and then that identity is rejected by the people I want to impress."

They may not say it that way, but that is what they are saying. This is what most of us have said at some time or another.

I certainly have.

The Kingdom of God is often referred to as an "upside down" kingdom, meaning that many things in it will not come naturally or as we expect.

Corrie ten Boom beautifully said:

"God's viewpoint is sometimes different from ours – so different that we could not guess at it unless he had given us a book which tells us such things."[32]

Through the lens of the Gospel, from a Christ centered worldview, learning to be ourselves is one of these upside down ideas.

Because in becoming ourselves, Jesus does not tell us to find ourselves. He tells us to lose ourselves. He tells us to die to ourselves and that there, in paradox, is where we will be most alive.[33]

The best self we will ever be is the self that has been crucified with Christ. This is the self the Apostle Paul wrote about in Galatians 2:20. This is the self that no longer lives for itself but for Christ who lives in us.

When I am in Christ, I have been adopted into God's family. I am His daughter. I am His ambassador. Being a part of this family, being part of this workmanship, tells me who I am and tells me who I am not. It continually points me to my true self, to my Gospel self.

As I walk with Jesus, I lose more of my self infected by sin, doubt, and insecurity and become more of His self – fully loved and fully devoted to the Father's will. As I walk with Jesus, He gives me my identity and invites me to be the full expression of who He created me to be.

This might be a "hold up" moment. I get the fear here.

Do all who die to themselves become the same self? Is the church to be a collection of clones – a pack of people who look the same, sound the same, dress the same, and remain the same? Is all this same…lame?

In the book *The Screwtape Letters,* C.S. Lewis wrote:

"When [God] talks of their losing their selves, He means only abandoning the clamour of self-will; once they have done that, He really gives them back all their personality, and boasts (I am afraid, sincerely) that when they are wholly His they will be more themselves than ever."[34]

More ourselves than ever. What if, by grace, that is what Jesus offers us? To be more ourselves than ever.

Such a wonder-full thought. Such a worthy, freeing thought.

...

Last summer, I did a sugar detox.

Sugar is my nicotine. I can chain-smoke Sour Patch Kids.

Put a bowl of candy corn in front of me, and I have the self-control of a 5 year old. So, when my father who had always been in great physical shape was diagnosed with diabetes, I knew I needed to change my ways and come out of a gas station every now and again without Cherry Sours.

The thing about doing a full sugar detox is it's not just about the soda and the coffee cake.

Sugar is in...well, EVERYTHING. #America

To truly detox, it means label reading. Label reading means wanting to give up and roll your grocery cart off the nearest cliff and your soul along with it.

"Wait, there is sugar in HUMMUS?! How did that sneak in there and it still taste like punishment??"

Basically, to sugar detox and eat processed food is impossible.

To stick to the plan, I needed to cook. I needed to eat foods not from a package but from the ground. I needed to fill my cart with produce, and for that produce to not turn into crisper drawer casualties, I needed to clean them and prep them right away – getting them as easy-to-grab as could be.

124

One day, on this good-for-me food mission, I placed the cutting board on the counter. I selected a knife from the wood block holder. I washed peppers and put them in a lineup to be prepped.

As I cut away their stems and bases, as I felt their different skins under my palms, as I placed their bright colors in see-through containers for the week, I did something I never do when I take a chip out of a bag.

I marveled.

The greens. The reds. The yellows.
The shapes. The textures. The tastes.

It was like the kitchen became a sanctuary and the counter held a stained glass garden. Light poured in through its windows, telling me a story.

"God is not bland," I whispered to the cutting board, observing the pepper rainbow, basking in its insight.

Creation helps us see the Creator behind it all. What I saw in that moment was God did not create dull. He did not make everything "samesy."

Like peppers. Like people.

In Psalm 139, David wrote:

"I praise you, for I am fearfully and wonderfully made.
Wonderful are your works; my soul knows it very well.
My frame was not hidden from you, when I was being made
in secret, intricately woven in the depths of the earth."[35]

Intricately woven. That is how God made us.

Our creation was not a mass production. It was intentional. It was thought through, mindful, purposeful, careful.

Our personalities. Our likes. Our dislikes. Our humor. Our time in history. Our place. Our dreams. Our purposes.

Dying to ourselves, abandoning the "clamor of self-will" as Lewis put it, does not remove any strand woven by God.

It eliminates the sin and self-obsession that snags and tarnishes the strands.

I washed the pepper, not to remove any of the "pepper" from it but to take the dirt off. To restore it to its best, to its wholeness.

This is what Jesus does for us. Coming to Him as Lord and Savior is saying, "Please take my dirt off. I want to be my most God-created self."

Even if the scrubbing gets uncomfortable. Even if it involves a cutting board.

The self that has died to sin and selfishness is the freest self possible, because it is controlled not by outside expectations but a humble confidence that loves God and serves others in whatever context it finds itself.

That will always be where we are at our best.

The self that is left after we die to ourselves does not have to impress anybody. It does not have to compete or compare. It does not have to talk itself up to anyone or talk down to someone else. It does not have to self promote.

The self that has died to sin and selfishness is at rest in God and resurrected to a self-less mission.

...

Have you ever known those people who are naturally cool?

Like somehow, whatever they wear, whatever they listen to, whatever they are into is just cool?

To quote *Mean Girls,* they are the ones who "wear army pants and flip flops, so you buy army pants and flip flops."[36]

One of my best friends is this way. So is my sister-in-law. When I describe Teen or Anna, cool is the first word I use.

They are army pants and flip flops.[37]

I, on the other hand, am not. I am what you would call lame. Seriously, there is so much lame in my game. It is part of me. It is my texture.

It comes out in how I love pun Halloween costumes and how I sound completely unnatural cussing. You'll see it when you find the game of Boggle I keep in my trunk for emergencies. I have been told I could cosplay Dr. Quinn Medicine Woman. (Toss another *Was that a compliment?* log on the fire.)

My dream "Girls Trip" is Colonial Williamsburg.

So, I'm not cool. I have no other side of the pillow. And I don't fight these strands of my personality anymore.

I used to. I used to try and gauge what was cool and then do my best to represent and match that and stuff down whatever did not seem cool. But that is exhausting. And fake.

127

In my 20s I learned: I would rather be lame and sincere than cool and striving. Not because lame is better than cool, but because lame is myself.

…

I liked this guy in college. Like, really liked.

I got nervous when he was around and in front of him, I took inventory of everything I said, hoping I did not sound stupid. I made up excuses to talk to him and put myself in his way.

I was not sure if he liked me, but I did know he liked Monty Python; therefore, I determined that I, too, would like Monty Python.

There is only one problem.

I do not really like Monty Python.
(I'm aware of the comedy sacrilege. #BurnTheWitch)

It's not that I think it's the worst. I just don't think it's that funny. I chuckle on occasion, sure, but that's as much as I've got. Unfortunately, crushes are not known for making girls more logical. They make girls do dumb things.

Like, go to Blockbuster, clean it out of Monty Python titles, and devote an entire weekend to becoming an MP aficionado.

That is literally what I did. I went to British Comedy SCHOOL that weekend, all in hopes I would now be able to drop a quote, nonchalantly look his way, and he would know I was the girl of his dreams.

Trust me. Working, "He turned her into a newt!" into regular conversation, is no laughing matter.

128

Especially when it did not work. A tragic love story. Nicholas Sparks material.

I looked like/felt like/sounded like an idiot. I wasted time, money, and a weekend on movies I did not even like for a boy I did not even get.

All because I had no concept being myself could result in things being fine. I thought for anything to be fine surely I would need to be other than myself or more than myself.

But insincerity does not look good on anybody, and we are never at our best when we are pretending to be something we are not.

My pastor friend Nic Williams says, "When you know who you are, you'll know what to do."[38]

I love that. Jesus personifies that.

Through John's account of Jesus' life, we get to listen into the conversation Jesus had with God the Father before going to the cross.

Jesus prayed, **"I glorified you on earth, having accomplished the work that you gave me to do."**[39]

Jesus knew what to do, because He knew who He was.

When I think of Jesus, I think of the most sincere person who ever lived. Can you imagine being around someone who knew fully who He was and never strayed? Someone who, down to the marrow of His bones, was not a "poser" (as we loved to accuse people of in middle school)?

When I am myself in Christ, I do not have to worry about the details, the roadmap, the big picture. The glory to God does not come from me having all the universe figured out.

It comes from accomplishing the work He has given me to do. It is when I most know who I am that I most know what to do.

When I most know who I am, I can truly be myself and see I do not have to spend my life binge watching British comedies or wearing a doo-rag or chasing cool.

I cannot tell you how many times I have sat in my car before going into an uncomfortable situation and repeated, "Just be yourself, and everything will be fine."

When I do not know who to be or how to act. When I am meeting someone for the first time and wondering how awkward it will be. When I feel faced with social pressure or uncertainty.

There have been moments when I am pulling up somewhere, and I suddenly become really aware of something I am embarrassed of.

It is usually at a wedding reception.

Maybe my skin is broken out. Maybe I feel like I have gained 10 pounds, all in my face. Maybe my head feels not normal sized. Maybe I remember something super dumb I said in the past and am paranoid everyone else still remembers it.

I think, *"Oh no. Now I am going to feel so insecure, and I would give anything to just go home and lay my oversized head down on the couch and drown myself in candy corn and reality TV."*

Instead, I park my car. I breathe. I pray. I remind myself who I am in Christ and what really matters, and I go inside.

And a miracle happens.

I laugh. I sit with my friends and ask how they are doing. I find other people in the room who seem like they are uncomfortable and invite them to our table. I request my favorite reception jam,[40] and dance like nobody told me I couldn't.

I am myself, and like knowing who I am is a hex that insecurity will not come close to, I have a great time.

At the end of the night, I get back in my car with a peaceful exhaustion from having such fun and then that feeling like I have forgotten something lurks in.

"Have I forgotten something?" I think, trying to figure out what it is.

Then it hits. Oh. Em. Yesssss!!!

"I FORGOT TO BE INSECURE."

Jesus can do that.

He can make the lame walk. He can make the blind see. He can make water into the best wine. He can make a single girl in her 20s – at a wedding reception – forget to be insecure.

Because, He can make a girl forget herself.

I have not found anyone or anything else in life that can do that. At least not in a way that can be sustained.

No amount of makeup. No number on a scale.
No plethora of compliments.

We cannot be ourselves by ourselves.[41]
That will come with knowing Christ.

When we know who we are in Christ, we will know what to do.

As recorded in Micah 6:8, He has chosen us **"to do justice, to love kindness, and to walk humbly"** with God in this world.

We can do that in whatever context we find ourselves, using whatever strands He has used to weave us together.

Be your most Christ-centered self, and everything will be fine.
Forget yourself in Christ, and be more of yourself than ever.
Then leave your insecurity and doo-rag at the reception table, and go dance.

Chapter Eleven
Apple Cider Vinegar for the Soul

I just got off the phone with my mom. We catch up a lot on Fridays, since that's my day off.

She asked what I am doing with my day, and I told her how I met a friend for coffee this morning, had lunch with another friend in the afternoon, and now am hunkered down at Barnes and Noble for an evening of reading and writing.

"That sounds like a perfect day for you!" she said.

I smiled. She is right. This day is all the "me" things.

Barnes and Noble is my fantasy private island. I love it here.

One of my greatest "I should not be annoyed but I am" crimes is when all the comfy chairs in the store are taken, leaving only the second-tier wooden ones.

I do not like the wooden option, because I cannot relax and enjoy the read when I am in one. I am too busy constantly looking over the top of the page every few paragraphs, waiting to see if the elitist chair hogs – who clearly did not care I was coming in that night – have had the courtesy to leave.

In college, my friends and I frequented the comfy chairs on the second floor of the Evansville, Indiana Barnes and Noble. We would pick out books we wanted to read but had no funds to buy and purchase a coffee and try really hard not to spill any on the pages. Then we would get lost in words and ink and the wonder of reading.

Every 20 minutes or so, one of us would come up for book air, and we would have a conversation, before ducking back under the word waters until the intercom announced the friendly-but-stern "15 minute warning."

Most every time we went, we'd daydream and craft conspiracy plans of how one day, we'd find the means to hide until closing time and stay the whole night in the bookstore, emerging in the morning after the store was up and running, the employees none the wiser. This was our devious bucket list.

I don't think it was because we had a passion for trespassing. I think it was because we could not think of anywhere we would rather be than a bookstore.

I still feel that way.

I am here today (with no plans to commit a misdemeanor), and there is no way in one sitting I can get through the four books I have picked up from diverse sections around the store. I just cannot leave something interesting on the shelf.

Remember Gus Gus gathering corn kernels from the ground in *Cinderella*? Trying to squeeze the large, greedy tower he had acquired under his chin? That is me in a bookstore. Minus the halter top and with pants.

After reading a few chapters from a couple and placing them back on the stack, I reach for my laptop to start writing.

After all, that is why I am here. To write. More than I am here to discover my Enneagram number or learn about Mindy Kaling and BJ Novak's soup snakes relationship.

I picked up each of those subject matters while I am here, because 1) interest and 2) procrastination.

The petite gentlemen next to me with a kind face and black, Rat Pack hat is eating some sort of fruit in syrup straight out of a can with a Chinese label. Like a driver being waived through a traffic light, he pays no attention to my red-light earbuds, intended to block conversation and promote focus.

He starts talking with me, certain we have met before. I don't think we have. I think I just have common features, because I frequently hear I look like other people. Never celebrities.

"Are you so and so's daughter?"
"Did you graduate from such and such high school?"
"Were you an extra in *Lord of the Rings*?"[42]

Nope to all.

He doesn't care we have not met. I learn about his six year marriage to a cold woman who took advantage of him; how Bruce Lee was his cousin; and how he has a photographer friend in England who has an in with the royal family, if that is ever a connection I need. Now that Harry is taken, I don't see that I will.

He hands me a bright, yellow promotional piece of card-stock with his picture that identifies himself as a "Master Healer" and tells me to keep it. He then holds up a book about apple cider vinegar (definitely not from my stack) and asks if I am familiar with all of its health benefits.

I am not. All I know about apple cider vinegar is if you boil it in a saucepan because you read on Pinterest boiling vinegar removes crud from stainless steel (and thought it did not matter which kind of vinegar you use), your saucepan will not be more clean and your house will smell like Johnny Appleseed's B.O.

Telling me about the healing work he does, he asks with sincere eyes, "What is your specialty?"

I have to smile again, because this chapter I am getting ready to write, if I had a specialty in life, is it. It is the most healing lesson I have ever learned. It is my apple cider vinegar.

I preach this message to anyone who will listen. I share it with pure conviction and tested and tried experience. It is not one I talk about sheepishly or with a fail-safe, "I don't know, though," tacked on. Because, I do know. I believe it is truth for everyone, all the time.

This is my first time putting it in writing, and I will try my best to share it like your life depends on it. Once upon a time, mine did.

...

Bad things grow in the dark. Good things grow in the light.

At first sip, it tastes more like a juice box than a rich apothecary. It sounds like an art prompt a preschool teacher gives her students before passing out dry macaroni, glue, pom-poms, and construction paper.

"Alright boys and girls! Make a picture of a bad thing growing in the dark and a good thing growing in the light!"

I picture an elementary school hallway where these Pom-Pom Picasso style images hang loosely from the walls.

On half the sheet there is a monster eating up the darkness, with a blobby speech bubble howling, "AHHH!!"; on the other half, there is a growing flower, bright petals outstretched toward the peek-a-boo sun in the corner.

The bad thing in the dark. The good thing in the light. It's simple enough for a 4-year-old to illustrate.

And what is true of monsters and flowerbeds is true of our human hearts and minds. Don't the deepest lessons tend to be the simplest ones?

As a teenager, I might have understood this concept theoretically, but I had no working knowledge of it practically. I thought the thing to do with dark things was leave them in the dark.

Insecurities. Fears. Failures. Sin. Shame. What embarrassed me about me. All the ugly stuff. All the dark stuff.

Dark things petrified me. Talking about or acknowledging dark things petrified me. I would have rather run into oncoming traffic with a blindfold than talk about something that hurt.

Approaching one of those dark issues was like coming up on a mall kiosk salesperson.

"Do not make eye contact. Walk briskly.
Duck into Sunglass Hut."

I thought the way to make something go away was to act like it wasn't there. But ignoring dark things is a little like ignoring a tooth abscess. It can be done for a while but not without consequence and not without pain. Eventually surgery will be needed, and the extent of the surgery will be in proportion to the extent it was ignored and kept in the dark to decay.

Because bad things grow in the dark.

I did not understand light and what it was for. That light is intended for the dark was lost on me. I thought light was intended for other light. My mentality was that light was where we displayed what is pretty, what is pleasing, what is impressive, what makes us look good.

Honor roll. Accomplishments. Compliments. Achievements. Maturity. Clear skin. Good hair.

Bring them to the light! Let them be seen, and maybe if there are enough of them, they will block out and overshadow anything in the dark.

It doesn't matter how many pretty things line our display cases. We all have closets. We all have things we do not want seen or displayed or known.

I had a closet full of insecurity and fears in high school I did not invite anyone to see. It was not because there would not have been anyone willing to enter. I was surrounded by people who loved and encouraged me and would have gone wherever I needed them to go. But I was dumb. I was naïve and thought I could keep darkness to myself until it went away and no one would even need to know I had it.

I remember well-meaning people saying things like, "You are too mature to care about what other teenagers care about!" Or, "You are too smart to get caught up with what other girls get caught up with!"

Like I was not capable of being hurt over what naturally hurts a girl. Like I had things figured out.

I did not have things figured out. It was much more dangerous. I just looked like I did. And that caused a heart abscess I tried to veneer. Covering up decay never makes it go away.

Throughout my teens and into my 20s, I continued to shove whatever seemed dark into the closet. Feeding the abscess.

If something hurt my heart – to the closet. If something embarrassed me – to the closet. Lies, fear, sin, shame – to the closet inside the closet, inside the closet.

Despite having lots of strong family influences and friendships and active involvement in church and small groups and youth groups and on into college ministries, I confided the ugly to no one. I bared the darkest secrets to no one. I walked with people on the ground floor just fine, but not the ugly.

I guarded it like the Beast's West Wing.

It took a break down, and it took counseling, and it took the love of safe people who helped me look into Christ's perfect law that gives freedom to uproot and deal with what grew, what abscessed, in the dark.

Have you ever deep cleaned a storage closet? It usually happens for me when I am procrastinating.

I have something else I ought to be doing and that seems like the perfect time to go through my winter wear in June or sort my bins labeled "Stuff."

The thing about deep cleaning is in the middle of it, it does not look like cleaning at all. It looks like a giant mess. All this sorting and labeling and knowing what to keep and what to get rid of.

It is exhausting.

To get to the turn around where the mess gives way to a clean, clear space – it is work, and it will make you want to give up a few times in the midst.

Sometimes, you score and find some forgotten money, an unexpired coupon, some stashed candy. But mostly? It is, *"What do I do with this?"* stuff.

Clean spaces never come by accident.

If you see someone with a clean closet, it is because they have done work to make it that way. They have thrown things away. They have kept a running Goodwill bag. They have taken shrewd inventory of what they allow in, and they have made it a practice to continually make a mess when necessary, in order to clear what needs to come out.

Hearts are like closets. They hold lots of things.

Good things. Bad things.
Light things. Dark things.

If we want a clean heart, the type David pleads for in Psalm 51:10,[43] it will not come without intention. It will not come without dragging its contents into the light, vulnerably making a mess in the process, for the purpose of being clean on the other side.

Clean hearts do not happen by accident. They become clean because their owner continually cleans them out before their Creator – asking, "Does this need to stay or go? Is this light or is this darkness?"

The more diligent we are to examine what our hearts contain, the quicker we can recognize and deal with the dark that creeps in.

What are the dark things? How will we know them? The Holy Spirit will not keep what is dark "in the dark" from us.

The Apostle Paul gives us great insight in the book of Galatians.[44] He lists the fruit of the Spirit.

It is a beautiful list. A list of light. You might have learned it in sing-song form at church camp, like I did.

Love. Joy. Peace. Patience. Kindness. Goodness. Faithfulness. Gentleness. Self-control.

Just before writing this list, Paul gives another one, in contrast.

He calls this list "the acts of the sinful nature." It is a list full of ugly words representing ugly things. He says these things – the fruits of our sinful natures – are *evident*.[45]

Hatred. Sexual immorality. Impurity. Debauchery. Discord. Idolatry. Selfishness. Strife. Drunkenness. Fits of rage. Sorcery. Jealousy.

He finishes the list with the catch-all phrase, "and things like these,"[46] tying off any loophole where darkness might slip in.

He does not give an exhaustive list, because darkness does not need an exhaustive list. Dark things are *evident,* remember. They are evident the way spoiled milk is evident. They do not taste right, and they do not settle well.

I can think of plenty of "things like these" – plenty of sin and anti-fruit – I have found in my own heart. They might not have made Paul's list, but they are certainly a part of it.

Addiction. Insecurity. Fear. Ingratitude. People pleasing. Lust. Lies. Slander. Prejudice. Shame. Manipulation. Apathy.

"Things like these" are what embarrass us about us. They are what we would panic to confess. They are what we craft excuses for and run interference on to prevent anyone from finding out. They are anything but light. They are what grow in the dark.

Dark things are evident, but they are not always recognizable. That is what makes them so damaging.

What gets us into trouble, what keeps us in the dark and on a sinful path we never intended to walk is we are capable of not recognizing them in ourselves. We are capable of mistaking them for light. And if we are wise, if we are after a clean heart, we will not rely on our eyes alone to judge the difference.

We have been warned: our hearts are tricky, even deceitful[47] – capable of convincing us the darkness inside us is not really that dark and therefore, does not need to be dealt with.

...

I used to work in an office that at first glance, you would not have thought a physically dark place.

It had windows on either side. There was overhead lighting. But the room still managed to stay dark. The only reason I knew it was because I would frequently go outside.

After staring at a screen in the office for a prolonged time, I'd get antsy, and the back porch would call for me. No matter how hot and uncomfortable it was in Florida's never-ending summer and how impossible it was to see my computer screen when the humidity gave it a steam bath and how I would certainly lose wifi once outside the house, I wanted to be outside – more than I wanted to use Spotify.

When it was not raining, I would gather my notebooks, pens, MacBook, and other random office supplies and form a traveling desk on the back porch picnic table. Somehow even the wood of the table felt damp, because if something gets wet in Florida, it stays that way the rest of its life.

I loved my traveling desk that looked like an office supply yard sale, but eventually my battery would drain, I would tire of wiping sweat off my neck and straining mosquitos from my coffee cup, and I would head back in to recharge and reprieve in the AC.

Often, I would be greeted with the same, dumb injury.

WHACCCKKKK!!

My shin - shattering on the huge, red ottoman in the very center of the room.

Trip on a rogue rug? Who doesn't. Stumble clumsily over a book bag that had not been there before? Happens all the time. But impale yourself on a gargantuan piece of furniture in the middle of the room? How does that happen?

When I cannot see it. That is how.

Like it had evaporated or become translucent, I truly could not see what was in the room I had entered.

The same ottoman I could easily keep my shins from when I worked in the office is the same one that took me out after my eyes had been exposed to light and were no longer adjusted to the darkness of the room.

Before going outside, before being bathed in real light,
I had no idea the room was dark.

That ottoman taught me a lot about darkness. How eyes adjust to it. How things that once seemed so clearly dark, after time, become normal and workable. How we are not always the authority on whether we are living in darkness. How light has a revealing, objective nature – independent of my perceptions or adjustments.

It taught me how something evident can become unrecognizable.

If you had asked me if that room was dark before going outside, I would have said, "Dark? What are you talking about?" and probably invited you to have a seat on the very ottoman that would prove me embarrassingly wrong after an hour in the sunlight.

Darkness. Our eyes can adjust to it.

It can become like spoiled milk we continue to drink, losing the taste of fresh. If we do not expose ourselves to fresh milk, we will not know the taste of soured. If we do not expose ourselves to light, we will confuse it with darkness.

I am not an authority on what is light and what is darkness. I don't think another person is, either.

We need a master light to lean on. We need the sun. And we need an unmoving, always accessible, bathed-in-daylight porch on which to sit and recalibrate our eyes to truth.

Before practicing the principle bad things grow in the dark and good things grow in the light, I had no idea how much Scripture has to say about light. It is *everywhere*.

I'll start with Jesus – which is always a good place to start.

Jesus does not just claim to have light. He claims to *be* light. That master light we need to determine if something is real light or darkness posing as light? He is it.

He called himself **"the light of the world"** and said whoever follows Him will not walk in darkness but will have **"the light of life."**[48]

John wrote that Jesus' light is the **"true light, which gives light to everyone."**[49] This true light of Jesus **"shines in the darkness, and the darkness has not overcome it."**[50]

The light I thought was light in that office was easily overcome and revealed to be darkness by the true light shining outside.

This is Jesus. True daylight. Coming into our hearts with a light fully overcoming – and never overcome.

And this is triumphant and brilliant and what we sing about loudly and often!

But while light is liberating, it can still hurt our eyes.

Jesus went places and said things and did things that offended people – that hurt their eyes. He dilated the pupils of hearts, looked inside, and exposed darkness.

As my friend Jess said to me once: Darkness does not seem so dark until a true light comes around. That was all it took for me to remember.

It is like if you thought your "Viva La Black Coffee" lifestyle was not affecting your teeth, and then you land in a photo next to Señor Crest White Strip, and suddenly, you feel like you have borrowed your smile from Austin Powers. What did not seem so bad before is suddenly revealed to be damaged and discolored by what is perfect and true.

Jesus came to clean teeth – to show us how tarnished ours had become. On our own, we might prefer to just smile with our mouths closed or hang out with people whose teeth are more stained than ours or slap on some veneers.

This is what the religious leaders of Jesus' day did. They were experts at veneers – looking shiny and bright on the outside, while being dead and discolored on the inside.

I have done this. I have put on veneers to present an insincere, external polished-ness. But Jesus does not do veneers. Ever.

He cleans, deeply. He restores, fully. He does not cover up darkness. He exposes it.

146

The way for us to be cleaned and restored is to be exposed, too. To open wide our tarnished hearts, under the authority and vulnerability of His true, saving light.

I think what keeps us from transformation is we expect it to be comfortable. The moment it is not, we bolt – sure the perfect love of God would never ask us to be uncomfortable. (We need only look to the cross of Christ to see how deeply flawed and unfounded this theology is.)

Certain that beauty would never come from pain, we foolishly keep our mouths shut to hide our stained, abscessing teeth rather than reveal them for the sake of having them made new.

Transformation will many times be crushing and unpleasant. I have never had a root canal (or for that matter, a teeth cleaning) where I thought, *"This is pleasant."*

The buzz of the drill. The tyranny of the scraping. The smell of the metal grinding on enamel. The ache and moan of my jaws, tired from being pried open unnaturally wide. The drool on the felt bib around my neck. The dentist's insistence on asking me questions when my mouth is filled with equipment.

It is awful.

Why do I do it? Why do I make *appointments* for this level of discomfort? Why do I sit there, under the practitioner's light in pain, in unpleasantness, in the slobbery awkward?

Because I know all the drilling and scraping and aching is for my good. The dentist is not harming me. He is helping me. He is healing me.

Healing can be painful.

There is a story told in three accounts of Jesus' life that makes me cringe and gives me hope. It is a story of bringing what embarrasses into the light, for the purpose of being healed.

It is the story of the man with the withered hand.[51]

Jesus entered the synagogue to teach on the Sabbath. People watched and crafted questions, because they wanted to "catch" Him. They wanted to prove He was not as great as everybody thought He was. They wanted to pin Him to the mat where the only means of release was going against the law of God.

Jesus, as evidenced repeatedly in the Gospels, is the great, holy escape artist in these scenarios. Time after time, He walks through their fires without being burned. He untwists from the tangled web they weave of misapplied righteousness without breaking the strands.

Try to bind Jesus, and we will be the ones tied up.

On this day, they saw Jesus, they saw the man with the shriveled hand, and they knew Jesus had all He needed for a healing miracle. Instead of waiting in hopeful expectation, excited to be spectators to holiness, their dark hearts found a way to make it bad.

That is another thing darkness does: it tries to dim the light in others, to make us feel better about a lack of our own.

"Is it lawful to heal on the Sabbath?" they asked Jesus, spewing their "gotcha" question.

I hear condescension dripping from their tongues, as they twist their pretentious mustaches. (That's not Biblical. That's just me.)

148

Jesus cut through their "letter of the law" mentality to reveal the heart of the law – and in so doing, their hearts turned against it.

"It is lawful to do good on the Sabbath," He replied, before He demonstrated.

"Come here," He said to the man. **"Stretch out your hand."**

I used to read this story straight through, without much thought except to the miracle at hand.[52]

But one day, on my quest for living in the light, in my hope for understanding Jesus as healer, the Holy Spirit stopped me right here. Before the healing had taken place. Before the victory dance. Before the synagogue mockers were put in their place. Before the man, healed of his malady, goes free.

I paused here and put myself in his position – when Jesus, in front of all these people, asked him to stretch out his hand.

His withered hand.

I wondered if he had always kept this hand behind his back. I wondered if as he walked past people, he tried to hide or disguise it, thrusting it deep down into a cloak pocket.

I wondered if this hand had caused kids to make fun of him and had been the source of his greatest discomfort and insecurity and shame. I wondered if the thought of bringing this hand to the light in front of other people terrified him and caused his throat to burn and his heart to quiver.

It is this hand Jesus asked him to display, and I wondered if his inner monologue was something like mine would have been.

"Oh Lord, please. Anything else. Ask me to display anything else! How about my other hand? Have you seen it? It is fine and healthy and not embarrassing! Or how about my feet? My voice? My wallet? Please. Anything but this hand."

But Jesus did not come for what is healthy.[53]

He came for *this* hand and others like it. He came for what is sick. What is decayed. What is withered in us.

The man responded. He swallowed what was embarrassing, walked through what was humiliating, and brought to light what was more comfortably kept in the dark. He did as Jesus asked, and his hand was restored.

I am reminded of this story when I am tempted to keep what is withered in me deep in a cloak pocket.

I might still ask Jesus to heal it, but I prefer He do it in secrecy.

That He would quickly and quietly utter something under His breath as He walked past, and I could bring it out and display it after healing. After it's whole. After it's no longer embarrassing.

What is kept in the dark might not be seen, but it will also not be healed.

What restoration do we forfeit, what grief and heartache do we nurse and keep clinched out of sight, because we refuse to stretch it out in the light? Anything kept out of sight is kept in the dark.

When Jesus asks us to stretch it out, to display it, to "Come here," it is never for the sake of shame or humiliation.

It is for the purpose of restoration.

That is what His light does. It restores. It heals. It makes right.

But first, it might hurt our eyes. It might embarrass us.

His light will ask us to display what we would rather keep hidden. It will ask to see our withered hearts, our twisted thoughts, our broken lives, and our hidden sin and shame.

It will demand we display our weaknesses, which often involves other people. Other safe people filled with the light of Christ.

Because I so want to live in the light, this is a little light test I practice. It is a 4 part question.

Is there someone in my life who knows…

1. what embarrasses me about me?
2. my greatest fears?
3. my biggest insecurities?
4. the lies I am most likely to believe about God and myself?

If the answers are "No," there is a good chance I am walking in darkness. There is a certain chance I am casting myself out of the light Christ intends me to live in through Christian community.

If there is something happening in your life you do not want anyone to know – that causes you to lie, to deceive, to hide, to justify, and convince yourself you can take care of it on your own without involving others, you are not living in the light, either. Our unexposed secrets and sins build a closet housing darkness in our heart – where bad things, and only bad things, grow.

There was a time in my life I could not have said anyone knew the answers to those questions. I was not honest with myself about the answers to those questions.

Learning to stretch myself out, clean out my closets, vulnerably open up what is easier to keep shut, and put on display what is withered for the purpose of being restored in the light of Christ, has made all the difference.

Early in my 20s, I proved to myself what I was capable of. I don't mean in the good way.

I'd proven to myself the damage, destruction, and death I was capable of. I gave sin dark places to grow. I wandered into suffocating darkness so deep, I did not know how to find my way out or if there even was one.

But to those who know their need for a Savior, Jesus always makes a way.

His way was confession. It was the opening wide of my thickest shame and longest kept secrets, and it was demonstrated repentance to no longer give darkness room to grow.

His way was His purifying blood spilled on my behalf – when I was His enemy, when I was still in darkness – that brought me back, blew the walls off the closets of decay, stretched me out, and restored my soul, giving me new life and a new way of life.

This way was HARD. And it was PAINFUL. And it felt like getting emotional root canals every day for a long time.

And it was the way to healing that really happened. I really lived it, and I can really testify to it.

One day, after the fires of sin I had started in my life had been put out, but I was still smelling the smoke and trying to sift through the ashes, I opened up and shared with my sister my biggest fear.

She is one of the greatest agents of the Lord's light in my life, and I had a harrowing question to ask her.

"Brandi, how do I know I will not do it again? How do I know I will not totally screw up and land in a devilish pit of my own making again? What hope do I have in the face of that fear?"

You see, I had not intended to end up there the first time, which made it particularly scary. How would I avoid where I did not mean to end up but had landed before? Most people do not decide to destroy their lives outright. It happens in increments. It happens when darkness goes unrecognized and when eyes adjust to living in it.

"Your hope is this, Whitney," she said so sweetly, so reassuringly. "You have learned to live in the light."

That was my hope that day and that is my hope today. I have learned to live in the light. Good things grow in the light.

I had grown in the light.

...

"This is the message we have heard from him and proclaim to you, that God is light, and in him is no darkness at all. If we say we have fellowship with him while we walk in darkness, we lie and do not practice the truth. But if we walk in the light, as he is in the light, we have fellowship with one another, and the blood of Jesus his Son cleanses us from all sin." 1 John 1:5-7, ESV

With Jesus, we can practice the truth of continually walking in the light – welcoming it *especially* when it hurts our eyes.

With Jesus, when tempted to keep a sin, to keep a secret, to keep darkness hidden, we are compelled to drag it into the light, so fast it would make no sense to someone who is content to walk in darkness.

With Jesus, we boast in our weaknesses, we display what would be more comfortable to keep in the closet, because we have become light addicts.

With Jesus, we continually clean out our hearts, exposing anything ugly and decaying in it, for the purpose of purity – to cultivate the grounds where good fruit grows in light and light alone.

This reality saved my life and continues to.

Bad things grow in the dark. Good things grow in the light. I am not an exception. I don't think any of us are.

In Jesus, there is no darkness. There is only light.

And that light is our hope.

I want to keep learning to walk in it. Learning to sit on the porch in its warmth, in its truth. Stretching out all that embarrasses me about me before it. Calibrating my eyes by the light of His word, held out like a lantern to light my path.

Withered things are restored there.
Hope blooms there.
Good things grow there.

Light.

It is His tool. It is His nature. It is the Master Healer's specialty.

Chapter Twelve
When All Means All

"The more we lose for Jesus, the closer we are to Him."
– missionary on a radio station I wasn't intending to find
but was meant to find

At 21, I had seven classes left to complete my degree. I was heading into my senior year of college with an established friend group, church family, worship team, job, living situation, and comfort in my surroundings.

Southern Indiana had been my home for three years, and it never occurred to me there would not be a consecutive fourth.

It never occurred to me I would not walk with my friends at graduation – that we would not take a group picture together in graduate gowns with a "2010" tassel dangling from the corner of our square caps, to finish off all the other group pictures of camping trips, Super Bowl parties, and late nights of laughter collected during college.

I saw the scrapbook before it started.

I thought we had been marching toward that tassel as a team, starting day one in our dorms, unpacking our Ikea furniture and learning to like coffee together, and finishing in the ceremony we worked four years toward, surrounded by family and celebration.

It never occurred to me it wouldn't happen that way, because it never occurred to me it would be necessary for it to not happen that way. My scrapbook took a turn. I had started making cuts I wasn't aware I was making, leading to a sin cycle I didn't know how to get out of.

Sin is a great salesman and a horrible master. An enslaving con artist. Junior year, it knocked on my door, took a seat at my table, and I ignorantly fed it lunch and invited it to stay.

The summer between my junior and senior years of college I stepped into the light that hurt my eyes – and set me free.

I intended to spend the second summer in a row in Chicago, interning at my sister and brother-in-law's church. Their names are Brandi and Neil, and I wish as a bonus to reading this book, you could meet them. I not only love my siblings, I love who they each married. What a gift.

Upon arriving to Brandi and Neil's Chicagoland home, it was obvious I was not there to have fun. This summer would not be

158

like the last one. It could not be. I was no longer capable of it. I had changed. Everything in my life had changed.

If there had been a scrapbook for the year prior – the school year between summers – it would have been filled with turmoil and heart sickness, terror and shame. No one envisions the darkest pages of their scrapbooks. The shameful seasons. The choices you want to forget and the images you don't want anyone to see.

The summer before, I had left excited for life and laughter and stories and memories. I wanted to storm junior year with passion and whimsy and full on expected to. I thought its scrapbook pages would be bright and colorful, good and typical.

So many unwise, darkened decisions and patterns set the stage and created the page for a very different story. One shameful cut at a time, I returned to Chicago a slave to darkness, confused by sin and having no idea who I was anymore.

I tried my hardest to keep the shackles under my shirtsleeves and cover up the rattling chains with banter and distraction, but I arrived at my sister's house carrying so much shame, it was impossible to keep them hidden. Of course my sister would notice when I wore long sleeves in summer, and she was going to hear heavy chains that were not there before.

When we continue shoving our secrets in the closets of our hearts, eventually, they have no place to go but out. They are toxic when buried, and I wore their toxicity like a sick perfume I could not outrun or wash away.

She and Neil caught the scent and cared enough to have hard conversations with me about what was causing it.

They knocked on a door I was desperate to open but did not know how. When it cracked, I fell through and broke into a million pieces – exposing all that had been rotting inside.

They picked me up, piece by piece, and helped navigate the purifying waters of healing and next steps.

I knew I needed to repent. I knew my life needed to change. I knew sin needed evicted from my life and denied a seat at my table. That was not a surprise.

In Christ, the opportunity to repent is always there. It's an open invitation. But the road to actually walking out repentance is not always paved. Sometimes, it needs built.

Repentance is not like standing on one of those moving sidewalks at the airport where we can stay still, not move, and expect to arrive somewhere different.

It requires deliberate decisions, deliberate movement – an eviction notice that requires follow through.

The more we talked, the more clear it became my repentance road needed to be built away from southern Indiana. To bring about radical change on the inside of my life, I needed radical change on the outside of my life. I knew the people on the outside of the situation would not get it.

I cried to my mom one night on the phone, as I prepared to leave Indiana and make Chicago home for the next year.

"Mom, I know this move – this drastic change – does not make sense to anyone, and I cannot make it make sense. It is my senior year! How will they ever understand without knowing the whole story? And I do not have the energy or heart power or strength to tell the whole story to everyone."

My mom listened and poured wisdom water over the fear flames in my heart.

"Whitney, when you take following Jesus seriously, there will be decisions you make that do not make sense to other people. Do not make your decisions based on outside opinions. If the Lord has shown you the way to go, trust Him, and that's all the explanation you need."

It was true. Following the Lord is not always sensible or comfortable. It does not always align with people's opinions on what they think we should do. How could it? As people, we love to give full opinions based on half stories. I do it all the time. Who but the Lord has the full story, the full facts, and the full knowledge with which to direct His love?

I am not saying we shouldn't seek godly counsel or listen to those who know us well and are filled with the Spirit of God to encourage and help us. That would be foolish.

In my case, the opinions of those nearest to me, who loved the Lord and were safe souls to share my story with and to look into my broken heart and give direction, all agreed: I needed to make a physical move.

Practicality was not calling the shots. True repentance was.

"Is this practical?" is not the question to determine if we are following where God leads. Obedience does not conform to practicality.

I think of God asking Noah to build an ark.[54]

Noah had no weather app to check the forecast for rain clouds. He did not know anyone who had done this kind of thing before to consult and apprentice under.

Arks do not exactly get built in private, either. He might have hammered away under sunny skies, as passerbys mocked and jeered.

"Noah's crazy," I picture gossipy townsfolk saying in the pub equivalent of that day.

"Yeah. What a weirdo! Who builds a cruise ship on dry ground??"

He did not build the boat because it made sense or seemed like a good investment. He built it because God told him to.

Noah trusted God, and what may have looked foolish to anyone who hadn't been part of his conversation with God, went on to save his and his family's life.

I think of Joshua's army marching around Jericho.[55]

For six days, circling the city, until the seventh day when they marched around the wall seven times, blew a trumpet, gave a shout, and witnessed the wall fall.

I doubt this was a tactic taught at their modern military academy. But the tactic burning in their hearts was: Listen to God. Be obedient to God. Trust God.

The Lord does not offer an explanation as to why He wanted Jericho defeated in this unconventional way. He laid out the path of obedience without exposition.

"Um, God? Wouldn't it make more sense to blow that trumpet on the first day and get a week's head start? Have you considered we will look dumb and no one will understand why we are doing what we are doing? Do you know an army is trained to fight...not walk around?"

162

The Israelite army was filled with people like us, so I imagine they worried about looking foolish or ill equipped to those inside the wall. Maybe embarrassed, they wondered if word of their marching would make it back to other armies, and they would be a laughingstock.

But Joshua had seen too much of God's faithfulness to question His ways. With integrity, he walked out the plan given to him to defeat his enemies.

God gave orders. Israel obeyed. The wall came down.

We can obey without knowing every reason behind what we are being asked to do and without presenting alternate options.

When God makes known His path, He does not turn and ask, "Now what do you think of that? Is that going to be comfortable for you?"

God is sovereign. He is perfect wisdom. We are neither of those things, and therefore, our opinions are Chuck E. Cheese tokens we put on the table in comparison to His solid gold.

There is a startling rebuke found in Matthew 16.

Jesus tells the disciples that soon, He must suffer many things, be killed, and be resurrected three days later. Understandably, this was a hard thing to hear from their friend and rabbi.

Jesus does not ask Peter's opinion on the matter but that does not stop Peter from giving it.

"No, Lord! This won't happen to you."

Jesus does not take it lightly.

"Get behind me, Satan! You are a hindrance to me. For you are not setting your mind on the things of God, but on the things of man."

Whoa.

Apparently the things of God and things of man are different. Very, very different.

The former will lead to death and resurrection. The latter insists on making sense, on being practical and comfortable, and can only be understood from the context of earthly gain.

How many times could I have received this same reprimand?

Whitney, build this boat under a cloudless sky.
Surely not, Lord.

March around this city for seven days.
Is that necessary?

Trust me when I tell you about the plan of salvation.
You do not need to do all that, Jesus.

My mom was right. (I am not surprised.)

Following Jesus and following the opinions of people will not be an aligning journey, and I will never regret banking on His gold over the Chuck E. Cheese coins of other people. Theirs might buy some cheap trinkets along the way, but His will lead to the riches only obedience can purchase.

Walking the road to repentance, responding in humble submission to whatever the Lord has asked you to do may feel like building that ark or marching around that city.

164

When the hammer feels heavy, when the days drag on and you have not heard the trumpet yet, my friend, *keep in mind the things of God.*

Remember He sets before us the path of life. He alone knows the end from the beginning and every hem in between. Those boats may be hard to build, but they will save our lives. Those city walls may feel tedious to continually walk around, but they will take out our enemies.

When He asks you to make a move that does not make sense, make the move. When He beckons you to give more money than you feel comfortable with, give it away. When He asks you to live in a way that does not align with culture or human wisdom or what your friends or family are doing, walk in His way. When He asks you to be honest when it will cost you something, choose honesty. When He opens the door for repentance and restoration, do whatever it takes to go through it. Break into a million pieces on the floor if you have to.

Take following Jesus seriously and when you do, build the boat, walk around the city, and pick up the cross. The crosses He asks us to pick up along the road to repentance will not be fun, comfortable, or accommodating to the thoughts of men.

Crosses lead to death.

They lead to changes we did not see coming and decisions we did not want to make and perhaps, the mocking of spectators and those who were not in on the conversation. They lead to pain and loneliness, exposure and suffering.

But in the way and beauty of Jesus,
they also lead to resurrection.

As we die to our reputations and our egos, as we crucify what makes sense to us and our reliance on pleasing other people instead of serving God, He exchanges our ash tokens for the beauty of a humble heart, ready to do His will.

Repentance and obedience build the boats in our lives.

Sometimes I look on the horizon of the church and see a sea of half built boats swallowed up by the sandy foundations we tried to build them on.

We start digging to build on solid foundation, but it gets hard and perseverance gets gritty and at some point, we decide it is a better payoff to play in the sand the boat is meant to save us from. I do not think it is just because we feel foolish building when other people do not seem worried about the rains. I think it is because we start and realize: building a boat is hard and expensive.

Repentance and obedience build you something,
and they will also cost you something.

Building and sweating and gathering material and persevering and picking up the hammer on days when you'd rather stay in bed. Looking impractical and wasteful in front of passerbys. Saying goodbye to land where you were comfortable.

There is a cost. Count it. And count on it.

When we surrender to Jesus, when we give Him access to our hearts and lives, when we confess we need a boat to get us off the sinking sand we have landed in, He is the architect and engineer of the whole project. He alone bears the authority to say what stays and what goes.

He is not like a contractor we hire to renovate something in our souls here or there and just leave the rest as is. He will come after every grain of sand in our foundation until we are built solidly on rock, regardless of how much we like what stood there before and what we stood on before.

This building and deteriorating process will not be pretty. He might not do it all at once, but as Lord, there is nothing out of His jurisdiction to shape, tear down, add on, and rearrange. Tragically, we can convince ourselves the cost is too much.

We thought surely when we sang and prayed lines like, "You can have it all, Lord!" there was an asterisk next to *all and *all would really mean *all the things we did not mind giving up.

Surely there would be things He would not touch. Surely there are sand grains He will overlook and enemy walls He will let stand.

The more closely I pay attention to the Jesus of Scripture, the more I realize all means *all*. He does not negotiate. He did not say, "Love the Lord your God with some of your heart, most of your soul, and a bit of your mind…if you get around to it."

All meant all. It still does. All of our hearts.
All of our souls. All of our minds.

When a rich young man asked the Lord what he must do to inherit eternal life, Jesus looked at him, loved him, and responded:

"Sell all that you have and give it to the poor, and you will have treasure in heaven. Then come follow me."[56]

Sin has never been honest with me about what it will cost to follow it. Jesus always has been.

This young man knew all meant all. He decided all was too much. He walked away sad.

Don't miss this: Jesus let him walk.

He did not run after him in a panic, realizing the sales pitch was too heavy. He did not try to strike a deal, and say, "Let's negotiate! How about you just give away half of your stuff? Or what if you put it in a trailer, and we'll take it with us? What if you keep it, and we'll come visit it on weekends? We can make this work!"

No. He let him walk away.

I imagine this young, wealthy man sincerely wanting to follow Jesus but being overwhelmed by the cost. In sadness, he walked away from the living God and the story heaven is inviting him into – and walked toward his dead, lifeless stuff.

He looked into building. He counted the cost. He walked away from all that would have been on the other side of giving his all, revealing his true god.

Whatever we walk toward when we walk away from Jesus is our god.

Here is where I want to insert myself into this story and run up to him as he leaves. I picture his shoulders slumped, his feet and heart heavy as he puts Jesus further in the background with every step. He trods slowly, hoping Jesus will change His mind and re-approach him.

I burst on the scene, out of breath from trying to catch him, yelling, "Wait!! You did not count the cost both ways! You only saw what you would be walking away *from* to follow Jesus. You are not seeing all you are walking *toward* by choosing to follow Him, by choosing obedience, by giving your all!"

I have sat across many coffee tables from many in the same position as the rich young ruler.

My heartbroken, conflicted friends confess with heavy spirits and sad eyes areas of their life that need bulldozed and sand-blasted. Areas of their life where Jesus is asking them to follow – but the directive does not make sense in our culture, to their families, in their circles.

There is a heavy cost, and they sway and stutter, taking a couple steps toward taking Jesus at His word and then taking a couple steps towards their dead, sandy stuff. I hear their pain, frustration, and fear. I know it, because I have heard it in my own voice.

We are terrified God is going to ask us to give up the thing we are gripping tightly, because we believe it is giving us life.

We want to straddle the middle ground. We want to follow Jesus and bring along our stuff. We want to pick up our cross and not have to use it. We want to follow Him and there not be a cost. But there is a cost to following Jesus.

It is typically whatever is in our tense grip.

When we want the boat, but we do not want to build it. When we want the Almighty power of God, but we don't want to surrender our all. That's when we want caveat grace.

I have wanted caveat grace.

Caveat grace is the heart position, "Lord, I want your grace, but I also want some stipulations."

It is when we add an asterisk to our *all.

"Lord, I will do *all you ask BUT not that. Do not ask for that. I will give you anything else."

The asterisk might contain a relationship we do not want to end, a sin we do not want to confess, a job we do not want to give up, a truth we do not want to confront, a risk we do not want to take, or a stance we refuse to change.

When the conversation goes there, when it is time to address the asterisk, it requires saying hard things.

It is hard to say hard things. It is hard to hear hard things.

When staring at an asterisk, I want to tell my friends what they want to hear. I want there to be another translation of the "all" Jesus asks for. I wish I could just give them a boat I have built or a friend has built or a great author or speaker has built, and they would not have to do the painful work of building one.

But we have to build our own boats. The encouragement, love, mercy, prayers, and counsel of others will help and spur us on – but we cannot repent, we cannot be obedient, for other people. It is our own feet that have to take the walk.

No one else can surrender my asterisks.

Taking the asterisks out of our eyes – out of our alls – breaks our dams of defiance and drowns out whatever we have been withholding from Jesus. Healing, transformation, and being made new wait on the other side of, "You can have it all," and meaning all.

One indication of a fully surrendered heart is when we come to Jesus with no caveats. When we are up to our necks in sand, when we are about to be choked out by all that is dead in our life, and we say, "I will do ALL You ask, Lord."

No withholding. No asterisk. That is when we know we are ready to build a boat – even if it makes no sense to other people. In my own life, it has usually been the caveat I am most reluctant to surrender that becomes the catalyst for transformation.

Jesus knows how to build boats. He knows how to make walls fall down. When He gives direction, take it. When He asks for all, give it.

I did not get the scrapbook I thought I wanted.

I do not have a picture with all my friends at college graduation. I made sinful decisions that brought in the rains and then I left to build a boat. Because of that, I do not have the typical story I thought I would tell. What I have instead is a story built of light and grace I didn't think was possible when I lived with caveats.

It is a story birthed on the other side of surrender, on the other side of making decisions that did not make sense to others but that came from the heart of God to redeem a child He loves.

It is a story that could not have been told had I continued to cling to my asterisks or made sensibility or earthly wisdom my god.

When the Lord shows you the way to go, trust Him. Do not harden your heart.

Ruthlessly dig out the asterisks in your life, no matter how painful the process is, no matter how entangled they are in your heart and how costly they are to pry from your hands.

Jesus does not tell typical or practical stories.

He tells beautiful, curious, redeemed, mysterious, hard, costly, counterintuitive ones. Let Him tell yours – with your all.

It will make all the difference.

Chapter Thirteen
Doing and Dreaming

"Now that you know these things, you will be blessed if you do them." – Jesus[57]

Mike is a friend who taught me the difference between dreaming and doing.[58]

Well, Mike plus a ficus and a lil' Photoshop scheme.

This simple truth has come as way too much of a shock to me: *having* an idea and *actually doing* that idea are not the same.

Wow! Brilliant! Who would have thunk it!

Thunking aside, doing – not dreaming – makes the difference.

I am not the most ambitious person I know. I'm better at coming up with ideas than executing them.

How many times in my life have I said:
"Wouldn't it be really cool if we _____?" or
"How hilarious would it be to _____?"

Then I laugh for a second, or congratulate myself on the good idea, and go right back to whatever I am doing. The thought goes to the ethereal universe, like a postcard with an address but no postage and no chance of getting to its destination.

Mike helped me see it is not enough to pick out the postcard. If it's to change anything, if it's to mean anything, if it's to get somewhere, it needs postage.

We worked together on a church creative team. Sitting around our communal desk one morning, drinking coffee, taking a few minutes to scan the daily news to debrief ourselves on world events (i.e. eBaum's World), we received an email from a coworker.

The email both informed and warned us someone had been moving the ficus plant in the church lobby. Apparently, moving it could damage the plant and was considered a high offense. It basically asked for the perp' to turn themselves in and repent of their foolish plant handling ways.

"Wouldn't it be funny if we took a picture of us moving the plant, Photoshopped it to look like security tape footage, and put up "Wanted" posters around the office?" I threw out there after reading it.

It got a light chuckle. That was enough for me.

Back to emails. Back to eBaum's. Back to Photoshopping for my actual job.

Whishhh. Mike pushed his rolly chair back from his desk and grabbed the church van keys.

"Where are you going?" someone asked.

"To get the van. Someone grab the camera. We are doing it."

This idea was getting postage.

Giggly, we loaded up and headed to the main campus building for our ficus endangering photoshoot. We got the picture set up by having a coworker dangerously climb on lots of things he probably should not have been climbing on to get a security camera angle. Then we Googled a prototype to get the timestamp and grain right in editing.

Mike even knew how to hack into our facility manager's email so when the "Wanted" image went to all staff, it looked like it came from someone authoritative and from real footage.[59]

The whole operation took maybe an hour. Postcard and postage in less time than it takes to watch a couple episodes of reality TV.

Except when I get done watching reality TV, I feel like I have torched the potential of my life. When I got done with this quick stunt, I had a memory that still makes me smile and taught me a transformational way to live.

The doing, not the dreaming, makes the difference.

Dreaming is fun, of course – and it is not bad. Dreaming can lead to our best ideas. But when we stop at the dreaming – when it's enough for us to just have a good or fun or meaningful idea and not execute it – we lose out on the impact, memory, learning, and living the idea holds.

How much goodness, how much world change, how many friendships, how much Kingdom of God impact happens on the other side of, "Wouldn't it be great if we…?"

Supplemented school supplies for children in our community.
Became a mentor for a vulnerable teenager.
Hosted a foreign exchange student.
Learned that instrument.
Picked up another language.
Followed through on volunteering.
Asked questions and listened to the answers.
Got to know our coworkers.
Sponsored a child.
Became foster parents.
Prayed.
Read that book.
Wrote that book.
Invested in a local church.
Studied the Bible.
Meant everything we said.
Had that hard conversation.
Apologized and reconciled.
Shared a meal with our neighbors.
Sat beside a grieving friend – to offer presence, not solutions.
Went on that coffee date.
Turned strangers into friends.
Started that podcast.
Put down our phones.
Gave when prompted.
Obeyed when we have no idea what is on the other side.

Said yes.
Said no.
Joined that team.
Took that class.
Planned that fundraiser.
Started that mission.
Traveled to that country.
Took an hour to make a memory.

There is no shortage of good ideas for how to spend our life, our time, our money, our resources, and our relationships.

In fact, Jesus has a ton of them – and will give them to us.

But if we are ever idea'ing and never do'ing, it is like taking a roll of pictures and not bothering to develop the film. What images could we capture – what pictures could we leave behind and have in our life reel – if we did the doing?

In the ficus heist, the developing looked like a brisk van ride, a bit of photo editing, and one person willing to grab the keys and make the thing happen. That is what stood between dreaming and doing. In reality, most ideas will require more than that, but the Lord gives us grace to start small.

The next time you hear you or a friend say, "Wouldn't it be great if we…" catch yourself in it! And start developing.

Get a date on the calendar. Make the call. Put in the PTO request. Start the group. Write the check. Have the conversation. Do whatever you need to be doing the doing of your dreaming, because it will not be the things we *thought* about doing that will shape our lives, our relationships, our cities, our world.

It will be the things we *do*.

The grace of doing over dreaming applies nicely to a fun memory with friends, but it hits deeper, more meaningful, more transformational levels, too.

Doing makes the difference. It is not a hard concept to see, but it is a disciplined way to live. Doing is a discipline.

Jesus did not just give us things to think about in this life. He did not offer opinions or motivational statements or pithy proverbs. His words were not intended to make a pretty poster or summer camp memory list, only to be walked away from and never applied.

I love the show *Inside the NBA* on TNT. I grieve when the NBA season ends, because I get so accustomed to hanging out with Charles, Ernie, Kenny, and Shaq through the week.

Shaq has a catchphrase he throws out to the show's Senior Researcher named Underdog when he wants to commemorate something.

"Underdog, put that on a tee shirt!"

I do something similar to Jesus.

He says something really good.
Really tweetable. Really noteworthy.

Like Shaq, I shout, "Jesus, put that on a tee shirt!"

Assuming if I wear the shirt, if I advertise His words, if I commemorate them, that will be enough.

Jesus did not preserve His word, His ways, His actions to give me things to screen-print. Rather, He gave me things to *do.*

178

God's word and Jesus' mission. They are full of directives.

To be clear, the work of redemption is bought with the blood and resurrection of Christ alone – through no action of our own. That doing has been done.

But the work of the *redeemed* is ever before us, and it is not for contemplating or talking about. It is for doing, much more than it is for tee shirts.

...

I am a writer. I do not mean in the professional sense or even the artistic sense. I mean in the practical, pen-to-paper sense. Hardly do I leave the house without a journal and a writing utensil.

To listen to a message or sermon and not be able to take notes would be my torture. I still keep and carry a paper planner, because my best shot at remembering something is when I have written it and can look back on it.

Frequently in conversation, I hear a great phrase/word/use of language and impulsively find a place to record it.

This happened one morning at my sister's house.

Having a slow start to the day, we drank coffee and put off showering. She told me about a recent conversation with her friend who is a pastor. He is someone who straight up *lives his faith* in Jesus and who I would always want to learn from.

Brandi had recently asked him how he counsels people – what format/strategy/technique he uses.

He responded, "Counseling is simple. Most sessions break down the same way with the same components. I ask:

1. What is the problem?
2. What does God's word say about it?
3. Are you going to do that?"

The weighty simplicity smacked me in the face.

I scrambled through the kitchen to write the words in my journal, the front of my Bible, the "Notes" app on my phone – wherever I could put it to quickly recall when I needed it.

Not because it sounded nice. Not because I am drawn to 3 step solutions. But because it was *true*.

There is a reason the 3rd question is not, "So how do you *feel* about what God's word says?" or "What's your *opinion* on what God's word says?" or "Are you going to listen to what it says?"

He asks: Are you going to DO what it says? Because he knows.

The doing will make the difference.

I am not trying to minimize heart pain and trauma. I am not assuming complicated relationships and messy situations can be quickly tidied with a Swiffer Sweeper of a 3 step program or suggesting if you are not "fixed" after a counseling session, you are not doing it right. That would be shame inducing.

Shame is not my intention, and it is never God's intention.

Redemption is. Redemptive work is often patient work. Gradual work. Sowing and growing and waiting and watching work. It is often gut-level honesty work, too.

The book of James says it straight.

"Do not merely listen to the word, and so deceive yourselves. Do what it says. Anyone who listens to the word but does not do what it says is like someone who looks at his face in a mirror and after looking at himself, goes away and immediately forgets what he looks like. But whoever looks intently into the perfect law that gives freedom, and continues in it – not forgetting what they have heard, but doing it – they will be blessed in what they do."
James 1:22-24, NIV

When we think it is enough to merely listen to God's wisdom and word and agree – we deceive ourselves. The agreeing will not make the difference. Doing what is says and *continuing* in it does.

I am not a professional counselor, but I am a friend. A friend who frequently has coffee and conversation with other friends. This was the case one afternoon on a sunny patio.

A coffee comrade shared with me about her unhealthy relationship that did not honor her or God. She asked for help.

This was a beautiful, fun, smart, and good-hearted girl. The kind of girl if you met you would think, "There's no way she would settle for a jerky guy! She could get any good guy she wanted!" But the heart does not play by logic.

Sometimes jerky guys are attractive (whyyyyy) and sometimes girls are more drawn to chemistry than we are to wisdom.

For further reference, listen to any Taylor Swift song.

We had multiple conversations all coming to the same conclusion: she needed to cut off the relationship.

She needed to not answer the phone when he called. She needed to unfollow his social media accounts. She needed to not text him no matter how funny the story or how jealous she felt when finding out he hung out with another girl. She needed to not buy him a Christmas gift. She needed to ignore his birthday as an excuse to reach out. She needed to be done and seek wholeness in a relationship with Christ before seeking it with any human. She needed to guard her heart at all costs.

But it did not happen. His force field was too strong, and she did not take herself out of it.

She would reach out and say she needed to talk again. We'd get back together. She would spill her heart about how bad the relationship was and how rude and hurtful he could be. And we would have the same conversation.

Nothing changed, because nothing changed.

With a heavy heart, looking away, she would say, ashamedly, "I cannot do it. I do not know how to not answer the phone when he calls."

To continue to talk about what needs to be done without any of the doing is exhausting and unhelpful. There are only so many ways we can get instruction on how not to answer the phone. Eventually, it comes down to…not answering. And continuing in it.

I am not trying to make light of heartbreak. I have picked up the phone (or even wished it would ring) when I have known better.

Relationships are complicated. Ending relationships is brutal.

182

But to detect the problem (*unhealthy relationship*), enlist wisdom and resources to pave the path out (*break off communication*), and then walk in the opposite direction (*answer the phone when he calls*) is a waste of time. It is forgetting what we have heard.

It is what James warns us of.

It is like complaining about being broke and in debt but refusing to make a budget. It is like hating being out of shape but not making an effort to exercise or eat right.

It will ALWAYS be easier to not do the doing.

Spending with no budget is way easier than being disciplined with money. Having Dominos on speed dial is way easier than meal planning, grocery shopping, and chopping vegetables.

But the easy route is not the disciplined route, and it is the disciplined route that leads to freedom.

My friend had operated as though a magic wand would wave just by us talking and either heal the relationship of its mangled, unhealthy roots or get her out of it without pain and doing.

Neither happened.

I have done the same thing. I have looked for the same wand and not found it. What the Lord more often gives is wisdom and the way of discipline.

Neither are magic wands.

They are more like bricks and mortar and shovels.
Building agents. Sweat equity.

The sooner we learn we are not an exception to wisdom and discipline, the sooner we can move forward on the healing, constructive, life changing, freedom paths they pave.

I have another coffee-talking friend named Katie.

Katie knows that path. She has picked up the shovel and moved the bricks. Katie is fun and kind – full of spunk, line dances, and life. You would love her.

I met her at a time when her story resembled so many other girls' stories. At a crossroads in a bad relationship, she had moved home to sort things out and decide her next steps.

We sat across from each other at "My Favorite Muffin" in Reno to talk about it. To say the hard things. To look into the mirror – the perfect one that gives freedom – no matter what we saw.

"Katie," I looked into her weepy, sinking eyes. "I know this hurts. I know this is hard. I am so sorry your heart is aching. But he has shown you his character. He has shown you what being in a relationship with him will be like. Has it been loving? Is it truly what you want? Can you be brave enough to look at the truth and not what you want the truth to be?"

Gulp. Saying the opposite of what your friend wants you to say is never easy.

She loved him, she cared about him, and she had a history of some good memories with him, but he had shown harsh, damaging tendencies. He blame shifted and convinced her every problem in their relationship was her fault.

She asked if we could talk about it over a bagel (my kind of friend), as she decided if she should move back to where he lived and try again. He had shown no signs of changing but

184

told her he would once she got back. I did what I always do when a friend is having relationship trouble.

I recommended watching Andy Stanley's series
The New Rules for Love, Sex, and Dating.[60]

She did. She watched all 4 parts – and listened and discussed the content. Then, she did something way, way, way better than watching and discussing.

She put its wisdom into practice, and I watched her life change, her healing start, her trust in God grow, and her story shift.

I think one of the reasons Jesus calls the way to true life "the narrow road"[61] and then tells us few will find it, is not because it is impossible to find or hard to decipher.

I think it's because doing is narrow. Discipline is narrow. Most of us do not want it. We want easy. We want dreaming to be the discipline. True ways are typically narrow ways.

If you want to lose weight, there is not a huge variety of ways to do it (despite what the "As Seen On TV" aisle at Walgreens says). There might be variations on the ways, but somewhere, it will still shake down to: eat healthy and be active.

It is narrow. It also works.

Wide is the way that says, "Wear this ab enhancing belt!" or "Take this pill!" or "Keep doing exactly what you are doing and just complain about wanting to be in better shape!"

Nope.

The way is *hard* that leads to discipline,
but it is available to us all.

The same is true of money.

If you want to save money and not overspend, the wide way says, "Gamble your paycheck!" or "Invest in a pyramid scheme!" The narrow way says, "Do not spend more than you make. Have a budget. Be generous. Be prudent. Be self-controlled."

Truth is narrow – and it is the only thing that puts postage on our postcards and develops the life pictures we all hope to take. I want to be about the doing. Don't you?

I want to walk the narrow way Jesus talked about. I want to be among the few. Because it is the *few* who are disciplined to *do*.

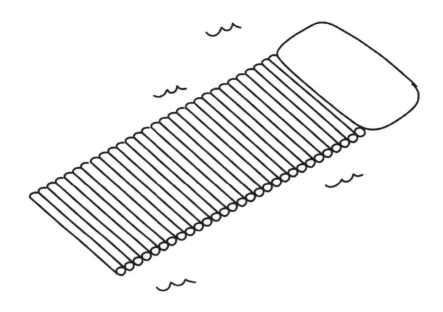

Chapter Fourteen
Exceptions

Toward the end of a small group gathering, my friends and I started swapping prayer requests, bringing about one of those conversations where no one makes direct eye contact with God, but we are all aware He's in the room, so we hope He will eavesdrop and intervene accordingly.

Sharing our wants – both deepest and surface level – I noticed a pattern, a cadence, a structure we all derived our great wish lists into:

"When...Then..."

When we get….the promotions, romance, travel, waistline, adventure, accolades, advancements, accomplishments…

Then we will have….happiness, contentment, joy, generosity, faith, trust, and peace.

This is how we believed it to be. We thought the virtues which ought to describe followers of Jesus were hidden not in the consecrated life and in the heart devoted to Him, but in the fulfillment of our wish lists.

That night as we disbanded and drove home, something about it bothered me. I couldn't believe it anymore. I knew too many exceptions to the "When, Then" formula. Their faces and stories scrolled through my mind like parade floats turning a corner. They were bringing freedom to an area of my life I didn't even know I needed freedom in.

These courageous, God-fearing, God-trusting Exceptions.

They have shattered that formula and shamed that belief by personifying peace and gratitude and authenticity and graciousness – while living without all they wanted or hoped for.

They have endured suffering and hardship and have received No's or at least Not Yet's to their sincerest prayers and silent heart cries and have maintained faithfulness, integrity, joy, and peace.

I know Exceptions. You probably do, too.

I bet right now you can think of someone who has so much of what you want…and is miserable to be around. I bet you can also think of someone who does not have what you want (and what they would want, too) and yet, exhibits a deep contentment and loving kindness.

Exceptions. They have been vital people for me to know and learn from. One of the most merciful things the Lord did for me in my 20s was introduce me to them.

I pray – sometimes with weak breath, a strained spirit, and a heart asking, *"Do I really mean this?"* – that I will allow God to make me one, too.

...

When I think about becoming an Exception,
I think about 2 Peter 1:3. It says:

"His divine power has given us everything we need for life and godliness through our knowledge of him who called us by his own glory and goodness." (NIV)

What a countercultural gold mine. What a soul U-turn.

Our culture does *anything* but tell us we have everything we need. There are entire college majors devoted to turning people into experts at selling us on the "more" we need.

Yet, I know people who have been led to the promised land of 2 Peter 1:3 – and have let God's divine power fill every gap their disappointments have denied them. They lack all they want but have everything they need.

Like Holly.

An Indiana worship leader with a big voice and a bigger heart.

Her worship fills the whole room. She talks about Jesus like a best friend. Holly is beautiful in every way a person can be beautiful, and she was single well into her 30s – a fate most girls would not choose and would certainly not carry with the awe-inspiring grace Holly did.

She carried it without complaining. She was not desperate. She was not in eternal despair. She worshipped God full out and pursued Jesus with her whole life. Single, or dating, or married with kids (as she is now), she has been one of the happiest people I know.

I do not mean a superficial, "I just saved hundreds of dollars by switching to Geico!" happiness. I mean the deep, bubbling joy that settles into someone's voice and countenance. I mean the happiness that comes from having everything you need.

Her joy did not unearth because God redeemed all her "whens" in a timely fashion but because she allowed Jesus to make her an Exception.

I got to room with her in college and witness it all up close.

You can fake a lot of things in front of a lot of people but a roommate is not one of them. Roommates see the real and raw of the home turf – when we are our most sincere self. Our pajama pants self.

In her pajama pants, she was honest about what was hard – and in her work, in her church, in her neighborhood, in the teams she lead and friendships she kept, she was faithful with what God had given her. She took God at His word and stayed ever prayerful, every hopeful, and ever fervent in spirit – come what may or may not.

Her Exception changed me. She had a different story, which she would carry differently, because she *chose* to trust God and carry it differently. That difference made her an Exception that deeply influenced my life.

I also know Pete.

We met as support staff for a medical trip to Haiti.[62]

Pete has one of those all-star personalities. Funny and smart. Humble dynamite. There could not be a more fun person to be around or a better person to have on a team trip.

After one evening meal, it was our turn to do dishes. We talked and laughed as he dipped plates in the tub of bleach water and told me about his family and life back in Wisconsin. I dried and put them away and answered questions about my home and faith. Trips like these have a way of making fast friends.

Something happens when you travel together, share meals together, embrace change of plans together, and live in shared quarters in what feels like 100% humidity and 0% chance of a nice shower. In Haiti, there is not much to distract from becoming a quick community. As a result, it is one of my favorite places on earth.[63]

That night in the mission house kitchen, I asked how he started following Jesus.

He told me how as a teenager, he lost his beloved sister in a car accident. He ran to God in the painful aftermath and has been there ever since.

I stopped drying the dish in my hand, stood still, and said the only theologically and emotionally appropriate thing I knew to say.

Nothing. It wasn't time to talk. It was time to learn.

I was stunned. To think of someone so full of life, so full of fun, so full of care and compassion for others – who has lived through such a tragedy. Someone I dried dishes with – who found the Lord in immense pain and loss, instead of finding only anger, resentment, and a hard heart.

He was not just Pete anymore. He was an Exception.

Right there in the Haitian kitchen. He was grace with bleach on his hands and holiness at his side. He displayed peace and tenderness the "When, Then" system tells us is not possible.

I dried this moment and put it away in my soul, knowing I'd want to see it again. When a tragedy, a loss, a "Why, God?" made its way into my story. When the enemy or culture or my own mind tried telling me I could never be whole again.

When I would be tempted to believe that along with what had been denied, I would also be denied goodness and life to the full because the "when" would never come, so the "then" couldn't either.

It is not true. 2 Peter tells me so. Holly and Pete tell me so.

One of my favorite descriptions of any person in Scripture belongs to the Old Testament character, Caleb.

God describes him in Numbers 14:24 saying:

"Because my servant Caleb has a different spirit and follows me wholeheartedly, I will bring him into the land he went to, and his descendants will inherit it." (NIV)

Isn't that what we all want to be? Isn't that who we all want to be around? Someone with a *different* spirit.

Caleb's difference is not in his level of talent or intrigue or ambition. It is in the way he trusts God and follows Him wholeheartedly – into whatever land God's Spirit leads.

When we follow God, we're not promised we will get everything we want. We are not promised to be the most impressive or best looking or wealthiest person in any room we stand. But we can all be different, because we can all have a *different spirit* than what we see in the world around us.

I do not mean different as in, "has a wild haircut, listens to underground dubstep, watches conspiracy videos on YouTube, holds a 'Free Hugs' sign at music festivals."

Yeah. Those things are…different, but I do not think it is the different God is talking about.

To be different in *spirit* is to be…

Someone who listens, when the world is so anxious to talk.

Someone at rest, when culture is busy and bustling and rat racing and exhausted.

Someone who is secure in their identity in Christ, with no need to impress people but wants to get to know and love them instead.

Someone ever learning instead of stagnantly believing they already know it all.

Someone who befriends without distinctions of desirability.

Someone who gives their life away, without hoarding a thing.

Someone who does not complain or criticize but builds up, works hard, and overflows with joy.

Someone whose operating system is not fear or worry but peace and trust.

Someone who does not live under the tyranny of entitlement but in humility, receives all with open hands from the Lord as grace.

Someone in her 30s who is single and still worships boldly and joyfully and talks about Jesus like a best friend.

Someone who is the welcome, life-giving aroma of Christ in Haitian humidity, when life has given reason to smell like death and defeat, but Jesus has given reason to laugh and trust and grieve with hope.

These differences.

They do not emerge from particular circumstances but from the Spirit of Christ, powerfully working within us.

...

I drove home after talking with a friend I had been trying to lead to the conclusion she needed Jesus. It did not work.

This was not some cold call evangelism. This was not me walking up to a stranger and handing a track and then watching them spit their gum into it. This was not me making small talk with the veiled ambition to walk the Roman's Road and then *WHIPISHHHH!* – sinner's prayer.

This was straight opportunity. This was a friend laying her busted life in front of me, and me seeing the clearing to voice, "Um, it does not seem like things are going so well without Jesus/faith/church/Bible, so what do you lose by giving it a try?"

Nothing. It was like I handed over a pencil, a pad of paper, and an instructional play-by-play of how to draw said conclusion and instead, she played tick-tack-toe in the margins.

Despondent, I sat in silence at a red light, thinking about the conversation. I felt heavy after it, and I did not know how to carry the weight. I am not typically one for existential combats, but this day, at this light, I kept walking into it, defeat landing on me like a grenade.

"*Does it even matter?*" I thought to myself, driving mindlessly when the light turned green. "*Would her life even look different with Jesus? Would my life even look different without Him?*"

The last question hung in my gut, and I felt the morbid curiosity to go there – to imagine what my life would look like without Jesus. I did not enter this mental arena with preconceived notions. I did not try to conjure up an "unsaved boogeyman" version of myself. My fear was actually the opposite.

I was scared unsaved me would not look much different from saved me.

I was scared what I attribute to the work of Jesus in my life (the fancy word would be "sanctification") might prove to be the fraudulent fruits of "self betterment" or a certain temperament or boot straps pulled up or having been born into the "right" family in the "right" place or a commitment to self care and proper boundaries.

I needed the answer. I needed to not look away. So, I looked. And I do not think I lasted 5 full seconds in the looking.

It terrified me.

Like I was floating in the sun on a raft in the middle of a beautiful lake, the question capsized me into the freezing water and dark world underneath.

I sank, opened my eyes, and immediately all the selfishness, jealousy, insecurity, and slavery of needing to be successful and liked rushed into my heart and filled my lungs.

The pressure of needing to "make something of my life" swallowed me whole and thrust me into a game of competition and comparison no one wins.

I saw the people I have gotten to know and the places I have gotten to go because of Jesus stripped away. I saw my compassion for people dwindle and my need for accomplishments teem and squeeze out character.

I saw myself make fun of people, with no remorse. I saw my heart harden to needs and stories around me – self absorbed and destructive. The world shrank and darkened.

This thought experiment was a reflection pool and my internal she-Gollum stared back. Her limp, slick comb-over clung to my veiny skull. Her gurgly voice haunted my isolation. Her big, sad eyes looked ravenously at what I refused to hand over to gain freedom – my gross, sick self.

Under the water I was the monster Jesus slays every day, when He invites me to pick up my cross (that kills the sin and disordered desires in my heart) and follow Him to real life.

Except now, with no cross to kill my slimy self, it just lived and grew and was miserable with no place to rest or change.

The murky water filled my car, and I wanted to drain it fast.

Paddling wildly to the mental surface, I took a huge gulp of fresh air and relief and hoisted myself back onto the raft.

The reality this "who am I without Jesus" business was just a fantasy greeted me at the surface, calmed my shivering soul, and offered a dry set of clothes.

My question had been answered. My heart rate was up. My mind had been transformed and was spinning.

From one stoplight to another.

My life following Jesus, up on the raft, has not been perfect or polished or pristine.

The filter still drops in my coffee pot, leaving more grounds than coffee. My skin still breaks out, and I get the stomach flu most winters. I have been disappointed in love, had friendships crash and burn, and taken losses I would not have chosen. I have gotten flat tires at inopportune times and needed an emergency root canal while traveling.

I do not encourage anyone to follow Jesus so that inconveniences and aggravations will not happen.

They still will.

A life free of trouble is never what Jesus advertised. What He offers is something different than everything being sleek, easy, and root canal free. He offers *different* itself.

Looking back on my 20s, the trajectory, the landscape, the overarching stories and character development: they have produced a *difference* I believe matters. A difference I cannot fake or muster or get from a manicure, a good therapist, and an inspiring Instagram account.

It is the difference that produces peace in the midst of chaos, character in the midst of "whens" withheld, and everything I need for godliness and life to the full.

This difference is why I encourage everyone to follow Jesus. It is why I encourage you to follow Jesus and why I encourage myself to keep following. In sincere moments of grace, I am able to see it clearly. I do not have to go into the water to remember what lies beneath it.

I stay afloat and can feel the difference warming my face. I sing to the music I am not sure anyone else hears. I smile at nothing visible but everything real.

This glorious difference.

It is what I would claim if I were in a court of law and asked to give a testimony on why I believe Jesus is the Savior He claims to be. It is what I would say if asked to defend why Jesus matters.

I would not start with apologetics. I would not mention the Dead Sea Scrolls. I would not make a defense for a literal 6 day creation. I would not point to a picture of Mother Mary some lady saw on her toast. I would not try to explain Scriptures that are hard to understand and put Bible stories in their cultural context. I would not "phone a friend" to a theological heavy hitter. I would talk about me.

My story. My heart in cultural context.

I would tell you what Jesus has made possible that nothing else makes possible for a single girl whose skin still breaks out and who still gets grounds in her coffee.

Contentment. Happiness. Difference.
Deep down, in every circumstance.

This is my personal apologetic. I have lived this 20s thing.

I have reached the end and will tell you I have met lots of people (emphasis on *LOTS*) of people who are:

More attractive. More thin. More talented. More funny.
More wealthy. More popular. More smart. More athletic.
More travelled. More impressive. More better and brighter and more beautiful than me.

But I have known very few people who are more happy.
I have known very few people who are more content.

That is not meant to be a braggadocios statement.
(Because, gross.)

It is meant to be a statement that points to Jesus, because if there is any truth to the claim, it has *nothing to do with me* – and everything to do with Jesus.

I have examined it. I have thought about it. I have sought in faith those whom I want to pattern my life after – those whose spirits are richly blessed, graciously different, and un-circumstantially happy.

I have dug down deep in their yards to find the source of the refreshing water they offer in a dry world, to uncover the secret of their "different."

With eyes willing to see, the Lord has allowed me to dig up the grace in the marrow of their stories Paul writes about in Philippians 4:12, 13.

"I have learned the secret of being content in any and every situation, whether well fed or hungry, whether living in plenty or in want. I can do everything through [Christ] who gives me strength." (NIV)

The secret is not in getting everything we want. It is not in ability, fortune, fame, followers, or tires that do not go flat.

It is Christ. It is contentment. It is acceptance.

Soul happiness flows out of deep contentment, offered by Christ's Lordship in our lives.

"When, Then" tells me contentment comes from happiness.

God tells me it is the other way around.
(God's ways are often the other way around.)

I see the proof in the lives of Exceptions.
I see the proof in my own.

Jesus has been the "then," when I have not had the "when." He's been the happiness result in a recipe where I didn't think I had all the ingredients. It is the best proof I know for His reality – for His life that is still alive.

It is this life – the content, different life – I am invited to live and anyone willing to pick up their cross and become less so Jesus can become more is invited to live.

In Christ, we do not have to be "more" anything for Christ to be more in us. In Christ, we have *everything* we need for godliness, for a different spirit, for an exceptional faith that produces an exceptional life – whether we get the "whens" or the losses.

Because we have everything we need for contentment. No matter what. All the time. In any and every situation.

"Godliness with contentment is great gain."
1 Timothy 6:6 (NIV)

Make godliness and contentment the aim of our lives, and "great gain" will be the recipe for which we never run out of ingredients.

Right now, if given the choice to have everything I want or to trust the Lord to dish out what is best, I would choose to keep following Him and let Him do the dishing. I would choose the unknown future and my known Savior.

I would choose to be the more content person versus the more "fill in the blank" person.

Contentment is not easier, but it is BETTER.

Live from your own "When I get this....I'll have that..." recipe or live from His "You have everything you need" recipe.

You will taste the difference, and you will taste and see it is a good difference. It is a good, sustainable difference.

I have gotten to do that in my 20s.

I have tasted too much of His goodness and seen too much of His difference to want what I have to offer.

Because I have also gotten to "taste and see" I am not good.
I can give more examples than you would need.

What I have to offer is the trash soup of trying too hard and
falling too short. What I have to offer is a she-Gollum and every
heavy, dark thing under the water I saw in my car that day.

Spoiled fruit. A cake with mayonnaise on top.
An undercooked pizza roll, cold in the middle.
A gallon of spoiled milk with a goldfish surprise.

I do not want what I bring to the table. I want a different table
entirely. A table like Christ's. Where He alone is at the head.

At His table, He offers a different spirit by offering godliness
with contentment, tapped from a secret spring ever accessible.

If I had to sum up the ultimate theme of my 20s, it is that
I am a horrible Lord of my life, and Jesus is a really good one.

That is the spring of all themes worth living.

I want to keep choosing it and let it choose me over and over –
whichever decade I am in. I hope you will do the same.

I don't know if we'll get everything we want. But I know we'll
have everything we need. I know happiness is ours for the
getting, because contentment is ours for the taking. I know
Jesus is the Exceptional one, making Exceptions out of us.

He taught me the secret…when the coffee filter caves,
when January comes, when someone assumes I eat McRibs.

The secret is always contentment.

The soul content in Christ enters the eternal surprise party of grace. That is a really good theme. And I am glad.

Because I, like parties, need a theme.

Sincerely,

A graduated 20 Something who is not nearly as insecure as she should be.

P.S. Was that a compliment?

Notes

1. I am not going to cite the article, because I don't think anyone should read it and submit themselves to cyberbullying.

2. It is a REAL THING. Most children talk about the day they found out Santa wasn't real. Wayne County natives talk about the day they realized "Bean Days" was not a national holiday. I just asked my siblings how old they were when they got the news. My sister said, "Sadly, junior college." My brother said, "Today years old."

3. Sarcasm

4. "Stephanie Gets Framed." *Full House*, season 4, episode 16, ABC, Original airdate 25 Jan. 1991.

5. No one is surprised.

6. Which is PREDETERMINED, not fake

7. Or in my case, what flavor of Doritos to set out.

8. Inside lines are out, outside lines are in – and cheap serves only score you dirty looks and a dirtier reputation.

9. AKA, the best sports movie of all time that's not *Space Jam*.

10. That would have been a great team name for us.

11. Peterson, Eugene H. *A Long Obedience in the Same Direction: Discipleship in an Instant Society.* InterVarsity Press, 1980, p 91. An influential, often referenced, beloved book of my 20s.

12. I.e. Discount, off-brand cereal bags the size of pillows. Honey Nut Scooters, anyone?

13. John Mark Comer went on to become one of my favorite Bible teachers and authors. In fact, the formatting and fun footnotes for this book came from his influence. If you've never read his book

Garden City, what are you doing reading this?? Go read a real book – like that one.

14. Not the most original nickname, I realize.

15. Acuff, Jon. "Should Humor Matter to Christians?" *Good Reads,* 12 June 2013, https://www.goodreads.com/author_blog_posts/4353262-should-humor-matter-to-christians.

16. Debatable

17. "In the Girl There's a Room", co-written by Sara Groves and Charlie Peacock. From the album *Tell Me What You Know,* released 2007 by INO Records. Sara Groves is my songwriting hero. There's no telling how many conversations I have threaded her lyrics into.

18. Any would do. Just please, not a knock-off brand with a rhyming name from Kmart.

19. John 11:28, ESV

20. John 11:32, ESV

21. Romans 5:6, NIV

22. Young, Sarah. *Jesus Calling: Enjoying Peace in His Presence.* Thomas Nelson, 2004. From the February 26 devotional entry.

23. From *Keep a Quiet Heart.* Servant Publications, 1995. per https://thepetersenpage.wordpress.com/2007/12/06/heaven-is-not-here-its-there-elisabeth-elliot/

24. Ref: Luke 17:21

25. Ref: John 14:2, 3

26. Ref: Revelation 21

27. While these are not necessarily explanations for pain and suffering, some resources that have been immensely helpful to me in walking with God through loss are the books *The Hiding Place* by

Corrie ten Boom; *These Strange Ashes* by Elisabeth Elliot; and
A Grace Disguised: How the Soul Grows Through Loss by Jerry
Sittser. Also, the sermon Timothy Keller gave following September
11, titled "Truth, Tears, Anger, and Grace", available on YouTube. For
spiritual warfare specifically, I recommend listening to Dr. Tony Evans
teach through his "Armor of God" series, also available on YouTube.

28. Really, are they the best choice for anything? I don't know, but
I was living my best 2014 life.

29. You can find the story in John 13-14.

30. Bless the "Plus One" girls. Clearly, holier than the rest of us.

31. You can access this 10 part series by searching under
"Messages" at onelifechurch.org - Part 1 was given June 2, 2013.

32. ten Boom, Corrie, John L Sherrill, and Elizabeth Sherrill.
The Hiding Place. Bantam Books, 1974, p. 160. If I could
recommend one book to the world, it would be this one.

33. Ref: Matthew 16: 24, 25

34. Lewis, C S. *The Screwtape Letters*. Harper Collins, 1942, p. 65.

35. Psalm 139:14, 15, ESV

36. *Mean Girls,* Dir. Mark Waters. Lorne Michaels Productions, 2004.
Line spoken by the character Bethany Byrd, who Regina George
punched in the face...and it was awesome.

37. To be super clear, they are not at all mean girls and are some of
the least "plastic" people I know. They are cool and kind - fun for
days. Teen and Anna, thanks for letting me sit with you!

38. I reached out to Pastor Nic to ask if this was original to him or if
I needed to also credit someone else. He said, "I'm sure someone
smarter than me said it, but I couldn't tell you who." I went with the
credit as is, rather than, "Someone smarter than Nic Williams says..."

There is a book on Amazon by Ronald J. Greer called *If You Know Who You Are, You Will Know What to Do: Living with Integrity*. I have not read this book, but I have read the title - and I like it.

39. John 17:4, ESV

40. "Somebody to Love" by Justin Bieber (the remix featuring Usher for it to really count.) I will judge your wedding based on whether or not I get to dance to this song at your reception.

41. I read or heard this idea at one point, and I do not remember where it came from to give credit. This is one of the problems with being a book, podcast, and sermon junkie. My money is on either Eugene Peterson, Dr. Tony Evans, Elisabeth Elliot, Tim Keller, C.S. Lewis, or Andy Stanley. When I'm not sure who said something, I usually say Andy Stanley, and I am guessing that is usually right.

42. I was not, but I do have a doppelgänger in *The Return of the King* so convincing, I even thought, "WAS I in *The Lord of the Rings?*"

43. "Create in me a clean heart, O God, and renew a right spirit within me." Psalm 51:10, ESV

44. The fruit of the Spirit are found in Galatians 5:22, 23. The version I list is from the NIV (because that's the version from the church camp song).

45. This list is found in Galatians 5:19-21. The word "evident" is used in the ESV. The NIV uses "obvious." The emphasis is added.

46. Galatians 5:21, ESV

47. Ref: Jeremiah 17:9

48. John 8:12, NIV

49. John 1:9, ESV

50. John 1:5, ESV

51. Ref: Matthew 12:9-13; Mark 3:1-6; and Luke 6:6-11

52. Pun always intended.

53. Ref: Matthew 9:12; Mark 2:17; and Luke 5:31

54. Ref: Genesis 6-9

55. Ref: Joshua 6

56. Ref: Matthew 19:16-30; Mark 10:17-30 (contains the beautiful detail that Jesus loved him); and Luke 18:18-30

57. John 13:17, NIV

58. Mike is also the friend that when I wrote to ask if I had his permission to share this story in a book I was self-publishing, responded: "You know publishing is dead, right?" I took that as a Yes.

59. Sorry about the security breach, Henley!

60. It is free on the internet at https://northpoint.org/messages/the-new-rules-for-love-sex-and-dating/the-right-person-myth/ - and I think it should be a human requirement to watch.

61. Ref: Matthew 7:13,14

62. I am in no way medical. At the clinic, I took pictures and handed out Swedish Fish.

63. If you are interested in learning more about Haiti or even taking a trip yourself, visit newlifeforhaiti.org

...

Illustrations provided by my talented friend and favorite amateur NYC travel agent, Liz Taylor. She is so good at all the art!
Hire her at liztaylor.contact@gmail.com

Photographs provided by my gracious friend Christie Mumm, Reno-Sparks area photographer and portrait artist.
See more of her work and hire her at jlmcreative.com

Gratitude

To God: Thank you for life and hope and joy and grace and laughter and goodness and salvation. If there is anything I said in these pages that is not true or honoring to Your Word and character, please chuck it from people's minds and lead them to what is.

To all the people who generously loaned your stories to the book: I loved living them with you, and I am grateful to know you.

To my family: In my 20s, you demonstrated there is nothing you wouldn't love me through. Thank you for believing who I was in Christ and for walking with me faithfully until I believed it, too. One day, I will know in full how much your prayers shaped a future I didn't believe was possible – and that I have loved living. You will always be home to me.

To my friends: You completely shaped the landscape of my 20s. I feel like the most blessed person in friendships ever, and I could list name after name, story after story, as testimony. If your name doesn't appear in these chapters, please don't think that diminishes your importance in my mind, heart, and beloved story collection. If we walked any stretch of the 20s road together, you are dear to me.

To the army of support surrounding this book project: You have been proofreaders, pro bono editors, coffee suppliers, writing partners, "How's that book coming along?" prodders, portrait photographers, sketch artists, design opinion givers, and top o' the line encouragers. You lent your expertise to my ignorance. You showed up at just the right time. You listened and gave advice. You chipped away at what was daunting and gave me hope it could get done. I am so grateful for you! The many, many you's. Mom, Dad, Jeremy Secrest, Barbara Hart, Mark Atteberry, Dianne Drinkwater, Julie Adams, Julia Seidel, Ana Cribb, Rachel Yancey, Deana Rogers, Steve Fowler, Liz Taylor, Christie Mumm, the SCF family, and Tues a.m./Wed p.m. Book Clubs. You were/are God's goodness to me.

To anyone who has written/formatted/edited a book ever: ALL THE BRAVO TO YOU!! I am so glad I did not know how hard this would be when I started. I have taken every book I have read for granted, and I repent.

Thank **you** for reading this book!

I would love to hear your *Was that a compliment?* stories (or *anything book related) at:

whitneywilson87@gmail.com or @whit_grammin on Insta.

Does not include typos or grammatical errors you find. Please no. I don't have the strength. Let me live in oblivious peace!

Made in the USA
Columbia, SC
30 December 2019